more Slow Cooking
Recipes

THE AUSTRALIAN
Women's Weekly

more
Slow Cooking
Recipes

acp
books

Contents

BREAKFAST AND LUNCHEON DISHES. 9

to 2 pints water, ¼
and ... filters ... milk.

Ingredients.—2 ozs. ... to 2 pints water, ¼
teaspoon ... salt.
Method.—Bring water and salt to a boil and drop oatmeal
into ... through fingers, simmer ½ to ¾ hour, stirring
occasionally with wooden spoon; serve with cream or milk
and sugar, or honey, treacle, or butter.

SCRAMBLED EGGS.

Ingredients.—4 eggs, 1 teaspoon chopped parsley, 2 oz.
butter, salt and pepper to taste, and about ½ cup of milk.
Method.—Beat eggs well, add to them pepper, salt, parsley
and milk, and stir well, melt butter in a saucepan, stir e
it, and beat well over fire until it thickens; do not
harden. Serve on hot slices of buttered toast.

SLOW COOKER

About the Slow Cooker

Comforting soups, stews, casseroles and tagines
satisfy and warm us, and the perfect way to master
the art of cooking them is with a slow cooker.

Slow cookers are available in a various range of shapes and sizes and
come with a host of features. We tested the recipes in this cookbook
using a 4.5 litre (18 cup) slow cooker. If you have a smaller or larger
cooker you will have to decrease or increase the quantity of food, and
almost certainly the liquid content, in the recipes.

The first step when using your slow cooker is to read the manufacturer's
instructions as each cooker will differ depending on its features. It will
also outline appropriate safety measures, like *not* leaving the appliance
unattended at any time.

Some cookers heat from the base and sides, while others heat just
from the base; some have timers that cut off after the cooking time has
expired, while others have timers that will keep your food warm by
reducing the temperature until you're ready to eat. It is about finding
what works best for you and your slow cooking needs.

A general rule of thumb is that high heat settings on a slow cooker will
cook twice as fast as the lower setting.

Brown your meat first

As straightforward as most slow cooking recipes are, it is best not to just throw all your ingredients in. Browning the meat first enhances the flavour and gives your meat a beautiful rich colour. Do this in a heated, oiled, large frying pan, adding the meat in batches, and turning it so that it browns evenly. Make sure there is a sufficient amount of oil in the pan so that it caramelises rather than scorches, and be sure to have the pan on high heat. If the pan is not hot enough the meat will stew rather than brown.

If you're pushed for time the meat/and or vegetables can be browned the night before. Once everything is browned, put it in a sealable container, along with any juices, and refrigerate until the next day.

Thickening the sauce

Coating the meat in flour before browning will result in a sauce that is thick enough to make a light coating gravy. If the recipe does not suggest coating the meat, then it is a good idea to thicken the sauce using plain flour or cornflour. Blending the flour or cornflour with butter or a cold liquid such as water or some of the cooled juices from the cooker, will help it combine with the cooking juices when stirred into the pan at the end of the cooking time. Put the lid back on and leave the sauce to thicken while the slow cooker is on the highest setting – this will take 10-20 minutes.

Another trick to thicken the sauce is to blend some of the vegetables until smooth, and then stir them into the cooking juices.

Liquid content

Casseroles, stews, curries and tagines As a general rule the slow cooker should be at least half full when cooking these dishes. Place the vegetables into the cooker, put the meat on top of the vegetables and then add the liquid.

Soup This is one of the easiest dishes to prepare in a slow cooker; just make sure the cooker is at least half full.

Roasts Whole pieces of meat or poultry used for roasting are sometimes cooked with minimal liquid content, especially if the meat is being cooked on a bed of vegetables. Sometimes a small quantity of liquid is added to make a sauce or gravy.

Corned meats These meats are delicious when prepared in the slow cooker and are usually cooked in just enough liquid to barely cover them.

The fat facts

When cooking meats over a long period of time they can often produce a lot of fat, which you will need to remove. The best fat removal method is to refrigerate the food; the fat will set on top of the liquid, and then it can be simply lifted off and discarded.

If you don't have the time to refrigerate the food before serving, then there are a couple of gadgets available in kitchen/cookware shops for removing fat: one is a type of 'brush' that sweeps away the fat; the other is a type of jug that separates the fat from the liquid. One of the easiest ways to remove fat is to soak it up using sheets of absorbent kitchen paper.

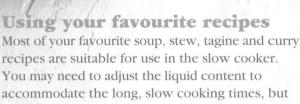

Using your favourite recipes

Most of your favourite soup, stew, tagine and curry recipes are suitable for use in the slow cooker. You may need to adjust the liquid content to accommodate the long, slow cooking times, but once you get to know the cooker, the possibilities are endless. For best results use recipes that you would normally slow-cook, well covered, in an oven set at a low temperature.

Freezing leftovers

One of the best assets of the slow cooker is its ability to cook a large amount of food at once. This allows you to feed large groups of people or, alternatively, have leftovers that you can freeze for another time.

If frozen properly, slow-cooked meals will keep for up to three months. There is usually a large quantity of liquid, so remove the meat and vegetables to appropriate-sized freezer-friendly containers, pour in enough of the liquid to cover the meat etc, seal the container, and freeze, remembering to label and date the container. **Handy Hint** Any sauce that is left over can be frozen separately and used as a base for another recipe such as a soup or a sauce.

Slow Cooker settings

The longer the meat takes to cook, the more tender and more intense the flavours will be; so if you have the time, set your cooker to a low setting. If you're pressed for time, setting the slow cooker on high will halve the cooking time. No matter which setting you use, the food will reach its simmering point. Some slow cookers have a warm setting, this is not used for cooking, but is used to maintain the temperature of the food until you're ready to eat.

Handy Hint The high setting comes in handy when you need to add ingredients or to thicken the sauce at the end of the cooking time. Remove the lid and add the ingredients, or the mixture you are using to thicken the sauce, replace the lid and leave it on high for 10-20 minutes.

Lifting the lid on Slow Cookers

As tempting as it is to check on your meal, lifting the lid constantly causes heat to escape and can set your cooking time back by up to half an hour each time.

Did you know? The condensation that you can see on the lid of your slow cooker is the evaporation of moisture from the meat, sauce and vegetables. As this liquid evaporates it hits the lid and slowly bastes the meat as it is cooking, ensuring perfectly tender meat and a wonderfully rich sauce.

The best slow-cooking cuts

Long, slow cooking will tenderise even the toughest cut of meat. Stewing or braising cuts are the best choice for the slow cooker. Tough cuts are usually inexpensive, but cutting the meat off the bone yourself can usually save you more money, as you're not paying for the convenience of pre-cut meat. In addition to saving money, cutting up your own meat gives you the opportunity to trim off visible fat and make the pieces a uniform size.

The best cuts of meat to use are:
Beef: topside, oyster, blade, skirt, round and chuck steaks, gravy beef.
Veal: osso buco, shanks, shoulder.
Lamb: neck chops, boneless shoulder, shanks, boneless forequarter.
Pork: forequarter chops, neck, shoulder, belly.
Chicken: any pieces on the bone, such as drumsticks, thighs, marylands.
Other types of meat: secondary cuts of goat, venison, rabbit, hare, kangaroo etc, are suitable to use in the slow cooker.
Seafood: is generally not suitable as it toughens quickly. However; there are many recipes for sauces that can be cooked in the slow cooker and the seafood added just before you're ready to serve. Large octopus will cook and become tender in a slow cooker.

A note on dried beans

Some dry beans need to be cooked before adding to the slow cooker because of a certain chemical they contain. Kidney-shaped beans of all colours and sizes are related to each other and MUST be washed, drained and boiled in fresh water until tender before adding to slow-cooked meals. Once they are cooked, they can be safely added to the slow cooker, just like canned beans.

Soya beans and chickpeas are fine to use raw in the slow cooker, just rinse them well first; there's no need for overnight soaking before cooking them in the slow cooker.

Slow cooker safety

Always read the instruction manual of the appliance carefully.

- Make sure the slow cooker sits securely on a flat surface well away from water, any heat source, curtains, walls, children and pets.
- Treat the slow cooker like any other electrical appliance. The cord should be well away from any water or heat source, and not hanging on the floor, as someone might trip over it.
- The metal parts of a slow cooker get very hot, so make sure no one touches them when the cooker is in use.
- Never submerge the base of the slow cooker in water or any other liquid.

Cleaning

- The slow cooker insert can be washed in hot soapy water.
- Soaking the insert in warm water and then scrubbing with a plastic or nylon brush will help remove cooked-on food.
- Check the manual first, but most slow cooker inserts are dishwasher-proof.
- To clean the outside of the appliance, simply wipc down with a damp cloth and dry.
- Don't use abrasives, scourers or chemicals to clean the cooker, as these can damage the surface.
- Never put a hot insert into cold water as this can cause the insert to break.

One-step cooking

It's wonderful to find recipes that tell you to toss all the ingredients into a slow cooker with minimum fuss or bother, turn the cooker on, let it cook away for the right number of hours and the result is fabulous-tasting food. That's what this chapter is all about.

veal stroganoff (recipe page 14)

13

prep + cook time 6 hours 20 minutes **serves** 6

veal stroganoff

(photograph page 13)

1.5kg (3 pounds) stewing veal
¼ cup (35g) plain (all-purpose) flour
1 tablespoon sweet paprika
2 medium brown onions (300g),
 chopped coarsely
3 cloves garlic, crushed
400g (12½ ounces) tiny button mushrooms
1½ cups (375ml) beef stock
2 tablespoons tomato paste
½ cup (120g) sour cream
¼ cup coarsely chopped fresh
 flat-leaf parsley

1 Cut veal into 2.5cm (1-inch) pieces. Toss veal in combined flour and paprika to coat, shake off excess; place in 4.5-litre (18-cup) slow cooker. Sprinkle veal evenly with excess flour mixture.
2 Add onion, garlic and mushrooms to cooker; pour over combined stock and paste. Cook, covered, on low, 6 hours.
3 Stir in sour cream; season to taste. Serve sprinkled with parsley.

nutritional count per serving 14.4g total fat (7g saturated fat); 1743kJ (416 cal); 10.2g carbohydrate; 59.5g protein; 3.2g fibre
serving suggestion Serve with buttered fettuccine, mashed potato or steamed rice.
suitable to freeze at the end of step 2. Add sour cream when reheating.

prep + cook time 8 hours 20 minutes **serves** 6

poule-au-pot

12 brown pickling onions (480g)
750g (1½ pounds) kipfler potatoes
 (fingerlings), unpeeled
1.8kg (3½-pound) whole chicken
3 medium carrots (660g), chopped
 coarsely
2 medium turnips (460g), halved
1 dried bay leaf
3 sprigs fresh thyme
1 teaspoon black peppercorns
1 litre (4 cups) water
2 teaspoons fresh thyme leaves, extra

1 Peel onions, leaving root ends intact. Wash and scrub potatoes well.
2 Place chicken in 4.5-litre (18-cup) slow cooker; place carrot, turnip and onion around chicken. Add bay leaf, thyme and peppercorns; top with potatoes. Pour the water into cooker. Cook, covered, on low, 8 hours.
3 Serve chicken and vegetables with a little of the broth; sprinkle with extra thyme.

nutritional count per serving 31.7g total fat (9.6g saturated fat); 2747kJ (656 cal); 27.4g carbohydrate; 61g protein; 8.3g fibre
tips For best results use an old chicken, as they are more suited to long cooking times; they are available from Asian butchers.
Leftover broth can be used as chicken stock in soup or stews.
serving suggestions Serve with dijon mustard and crusty bread to mop up the juices.
not suitable to freeze

poule-au-pot

prep + cook time 6 hours 20 minutes **serves** 4

poached chicken with soy and sesame

nutritional count per serving
52.9g total fat (13.7g saturated fat);
3361kJ (804 cal); 22.7g carbohydrate;
45.5g protein; 1.5g fibre
note Chinese cooking wine is also known
as chinese rice wine or shao hsing wine;
dry sherry can be used instead.
serving suggestion Serve with steamed
noodles or rice.
suitable to freeze at the end of step 1.

1.6kg (3¼-pound) whole chicken
5cm (2-inch) piece fresh ginger (25g),
  sliced thinly
4 cloves garlic, halved
2 star anise
2 cinnamon sticks
1 cup (250ml) light soy sauce
1 cup (250ml) chinese cooking wine
⅓ cup (75g) white (granulated) sugar
1 litre (4 cups) water

⅓ cup (80ml) light soy sauce, extra
2 teaspoons sesame oil
2 cloves garlic, cut into matchsticks
2.5cm (1-inch) piece fresh ginger (15g),
  cut into matchsticks
2 fresh long red chillies, sliced thinly
⅓ cup (80ml) peanut oil
4 green onions (scallions), sliced thinly
½ cup loosely packed fresh coriander
  (cilantro) leaves

1 Trim excess fat from chicken. Place chicken in 4.5-litre (18-cup) slow cooker.
   Add sliced ginger, halved garlic, star anise, cinnamon, sauce, wine, sugar and
   the water to cooker. Cook, covered, on low, 6 hours. Remove chicken from
   cooker; discard poaching liquid.
2 Cut chicken into 12 pieces; place on heatproof platter. Drizzle extra sauce and
   sesame oil over chicken; sprinkle with garlic and ginger matchsticks and chilli.
3 Heat peanut oil in small saucepan, over medium heat, until very hot; carefully
   drizzle over chicken. Top with onion and coriander.

prep + cook time 6 hours 40 minutes serves 4

greek lamb stifado

nutritional count per serving
20.6g total fat (10.7g saturated fat);
2207kJ (528 cal); 18.2g carbohydrate;
59.8g protein; 3.8g fibre
tip To peel pickling onions, place them in a heatproof bowl, cover with boiling water; stand 2 minutes, drain. The skins will slip off easily.
serving suggestion Serve with mashed potato.
suitable to freeze at the end of step 2.

1kg (2 pounds) boneless lamb shoulder
2 tablespoons plain (all-purpose) flour
800g (1½ pounds) brown pickling onions
4 cloves garlic, chopped finely
2 fresh bay leaves
1 sprig fresh rosemary
1 sprig rigani (greek dried oregano)
1 cinnamon stick

1 teaspoon ground cumin
2 whole cloves
2 tablespoons red wine vinegar
2 tablespoons tomato paste
½ cup (125ml) dry red wine
2 cups (500ml) chicken stock
100g (3 ounces) fetta cheese, crumbled

Stifado is a meat stew, usually lamb or beef, full of sweet baby onions in a rich red wine sauce.

1 Cut lamb into 5cm (2-inch) pieces. Toss lamb in flour to coat, shake off excess; place in 4.5-litre (18-cup) slow cooker. Sprinkle lamb evenly with excess flour.
2 Peel onions, leaving root ends intact. Add onions, garlic, herbs and spices to cooker. Pour over combined vinegar, paste, wine and stock. Cook, covered, on low, 6 hours. Discard bay leaves, rosemary, rigani, cinnamon and cloves. Season to taste.
3 Serve sprinkled with cheese and extra rigani.

prep + cook time 8 hours 20 minutes
serves 8

choucroute

1 tablespoon juniper berries

2 teaspoons caraway seeds

1 dried bay leaf

10 sprigs fresh flat-leaf parsley

800g (1½ pounds) canned sauerkraut,
  rinsed, drained

2 cups (500ml) salt-reduced chicken stock

½ cup (125ml) dry white wine

1 ham hock (1kg)

4 rindless bacon slices (260g), sliced
  thickly

160g (5 ounces) mild hungarian salami,
  sliced thickly

800g (1½ pounds) medium potatoes,
  unpeeled, halved

2 tablespoons coarsely chopped fresh
  flat-leaf parsley

1 Tie juniper berries, seeds, bay leaf and parsley sprigs in muslin.
2 Combine sauerkraut, stock, wine and muslin bag in 4.5-litre (18-cup) slow cooker. Add hock, bacon and salami, pushing down into sauerkraut; top with potato. Cook, covered, on low, 8 hours.
3 Discard muslin bag; season to taste. Serve sprinkled with chopped parsley.

nutritional count per serving 20.5g total fat (7.5g saturated fat); 1593kJ (381 cal); 15.6g carbohydrate; 28.8g protein; 4.8g fibre
not suitable to freeze

While traditionally a German and Eastern European dish, sauerkraut was widely adopted by the people of Alsace, the French region situated on the northeast border with Germany and Switzerland. Alsatian sauerkraut (choucroute) has wine, sausages and juniper berries added to the fermented cabbage mixture.

prep + cook time 6 hours 30 minutes (+ standing) **serves** 4

chicken, porcini and barley soup

1 Place porcini in small heatproof bowl, cover with the water; stand about 15 minutes or until softened. Drain, reserve porcini and soaking liquid.

2 Meanwhile, discard as much skin as possible from chicken. Place chicken, onion, garlic, stock, barley, rosemary, thyme, parsnip, kumara, celery, swiss brown mushrooms, porcini mushrooms and strained soaking liquid into 4.5-litre (18-cup) slow cooker. Cook, covered, on low, 6 hours.

3 Remove chicken from cooker. When cool enough to handle, remove meat from bone; shred coarsely. Discard bones. Return meat to cooker; season to taste. Serve sprinkled with parsley.

nutritional count per serving 9.4g total fat (3g saturated fat); 1488kJ (356 cal); 38.9g carbohydrate; 29.2g protein; 8.4g fibre
suitable to freeze at the end of step 3; sprinkle with parsley after reheating.

20g (¾ ounce) dried porcini mushrooms
1 cup (250ml) boiling water
2 chicken marylands (700g)
1 medium brown onion (150g), chopped finely
2 cloves garlic, crushed
1 litre (4 cups) chicken stock
½ cup (100g) pearl barley
1 sprig fresh rosemary
1 sprig fresh thyme
1 medium parsnip (250g), chopped finely
1 small kumara (orange sweet potato) (250g), chopped finely
2 stalks celery (300g), trimmed, chopped finely
250g (8 ounces) swiss brown mushrooms, quartered
½ cup finely chopped fresh flat-leaf parsley

prep + cook time 6 hours 45 minutes **serves** 4

moroccan-style vegetable stew with harissa

nutritional count per serving
12.2g total fat (5.3g saturated fat);
1659kJ (397 cal); 52.1g carbohydrate;
13.4g protein; 11.9g fibre
serving suggestion Serve with buttered couscous.
not suitable to freeze

1 medium red onion (170g),
  chopped coarsely
4 cloves garlic, quartered
2 teaspoons each ground cumin,
  coriander and sweet paprika
1 fresh long red chilli, chopped finely
½ cup loosely packed fresh flat-leaf parsley
  leaves and stalks, chopped coarsely
1 cup loosely packed fresh coriander leaves
  and stalks (cilantro), chopped coarsely
2 cups (500ml) vegetable stock

4 baby eggplant (240g), chopped coarsely
4 small zucchini (360g), chopped coarsely
2 small parsnips (240g), chopped coarsely
2 medium carrots (240g), halved
  lengthways, then halved crossways
¼ medium butternut pumpkin (500g),
  skin on, cut into 8 pieces
2 medium potatoes (400g), quartered
2 tablespoons honey
1 cup (280g) greek-style yogurt
2 tablespoons mild harissa sauce
⅓ cup loosely packed fresh coriander
  leaves (cilantro), extra

1 Blend or process onion, garlic and spices until smooth. Combine paste with chilli, herbs and stock in large jug.
2 Combine vegetables and stock mixture in 4.5-litre (18-cup) slow cooker. Cook, covered, on low, 6 hours. Stir in honey; season to taste.
3 Serve vegetables and sauce topped with yogurt, harissa and extra coriander.

prep + cook time 8 hours 20 minutes serves 6

mexican pull-apart pork

nutritional count per serving
26.3g total fat (13.2g saturated fat);
2842kJ (680 cal); 66.5g carbohydrate;
42.5g protein; 5.4g fibre
tip You can quickly peel the capsicum
with a vegetable peeler if you don't like
the skin peeling off when it's cooked.
suitable to freeze at the end of step 2.

2 medium red capsicums (bell peppers)
  (400g), sliced thinly
2 medium brown onions (300g), sliced thinly
375g (12 ounces) bottled chunky mild
  tomato salsa
1 cup (280g) barbecue sauce
4 cloves garlic, crushed

3 teaspoons ground cumin
2 teaspoons cayenne pepper
1 teaspoon dried oregano
1kg (2-pound) boneless pork shoulder
12 large flour tortillas
1 cup (240g) sour cream
1 cup coarsely chopped fresh coriander
  (cilantro)

1 Combine capsicum, onion, salsa, sauce, garlic, spices and oregano in 4.5-litre
   (18-cup) slow cooker; add pork, turn to coat in mixture. Cook, covered, on
   low, 8 hours.
2 Carefully remove pork from cooker; shred meat using two forks. Return pork
   to cooker; stir gently. Season to taste.
3 Divide pork between tortillas. Serve topped with sour cream and coriander,
   and accompany with lime wedges.

prep + cook time 8 hours 20 minutes
serves 6

braised asian-style beef ribs

2kg (4 pounds) racks beef short ribs
½ cup (190g) hoisin sauce
¼ cup (60ml) salt-reduced soy sauce
¼ cup (60ml) mirin
2 x 3cm (1¼-inch) strips orange rind
½ cup (90g) honey
5cm (2-inch) piece fresh ginger (25g) grated
3 cloves garlic, crushed
1 fresh long red chilli, sliced thinly
2 teaspoons sesame oil

1 Cut rib racks into pieces to fit into 4.5-litre (18-cup) slow cooker; place ribs in cooker. Combine remaining ingredients in large jug; pour sauce over ribs. Cook, covered, on low, 8 hours. Season to taste.
2 Cut ribs into serving-sized pieces; serve with sauce.

nutritional count per serving 15g total fat (5.7g saturated fat); 1622kJ (388 cal); 25g carbohydrate; 35.1g protein; 3.8g fibre
tip Get your butcher to cut the ribs so that they will fit into your slow cooker.
not suitable to freeze

prep + cook time 6 hours 20 minutes
makes 6

shredded beef tacos

1 Rub beef with combined spices; place in 4.5-litre (18-cup) slow cooker. Pour over combined stock, paste, chilli and garlic. Cook, covered, on low, 6 hours.
2 Remove beef from cooker. When cool enough to handle, shred meat coarsely using two forks. Discard half the liquid from slow cooker. Return meat to cooker; season to taste.
3 Serve shredded beef in tortillas.

nutritional count per serving 8.2g total fat (2.5g saturated fat); 1354kJ (324 cal); 18.9g carbohydrate; 42.4g protein; 1.6g fibre
serving suggestion Serve with guacamole, tomato salsa, grated cheese, sour cream, shredded lettuce and fresh coriander (cilantro) leaves.
suitable to freeze at the end of step 2.

1kg (2-pound) piece beef chuck steak
¼ teaspoon chilli powder
1 teaspoon each ground cumin, coriander
 and smoked paprika
1 cup (250ml) beef stock
2 tablespoons tomato paste
1 fresh long red chilli, sliced thinly
2 cloves garlic, crushed
6 large flour tortillas, warmed

shredded lamb and pumpkin soup
(recipe page 30)

prep + cook time 6 hours 30 minutes **serves** 4

shredded lamb and pumpkin soup

(photograph page 29)

½ cup (100g) dried brown lentils

3 french-trimmed lamb shanks (750g)

2 tablespoons moroccan seasoning

500g (1 pound) pumpkin, chopped coarsely

1 litre (4 cups) chicken stock

400g (12½ ounces) canned diced tomatoes

400g (12½ ounces) canned chickpeas
(garbanzo beans), rinsed, drained

½ cup finely chopped fresh flat-leaf parsley

1 Rinse lentils under cold water until water runs clear; drain.

2 Combine lamb shanks, seasoning, pumpkin, stock, undrained tomatoes, chickpeas and lentils in 4.5-litre (18-cup) slow cooker. Cook, covered, on low, 6 hours.

3 Remove lamb from cooker. When cool enough to handle, remove meat from bones; shred coarsely. Discard bones. Return meat to cooker; season to taste. Serve sprinkled with parsley.

nutritional count per serving 13g total fat (5.4g saturated fat); 1797kJ (430 cal); 34.7g carbohydrate; 39.7g protein; 10.3g fibre
serving suggestion Serve with a dollop of thick yogurt.
suitable to freeze at the end of step 3; sprinkle with parsley after reheating.

prep + cook time 6 hours 30 minutes **serves** 4

spicy lentil soup

½ cup (100g) dried red lentils

1 litre (4 cups) chicken stock

400g (12½ ounces) canned diced
tomatoes

2 dried bay leaves

3 cloves garlic, crushed

¾ cup (100g) mild indian curry paste

2 small carrots (240g), chopped coarsely

1 stalk celery (150g), trimmed, sliced
thinly

2 medium potatoes (400g),
chopped coarsely

½ cup (140g) greek-style yogurt

½ cup finely chopped fresh coriander
(cilantro)

1 Rinse lentils under cold water until water runs clear; drain.

2 Combine lentils, stock, undrained tomatoes, bay leaves, garlic, paste, carrot, celery and potato in 4.5-litre (18-cup) slow cooker. Cook, covered, on low, 6 hours. Season to taste.

3 Serve soup topped with yogurt and coriander.

nutritional count per serving 12.5g total fat (3.4g saturated fat); 1421kJ (340 cal); 36.2g carbohydrate; 15.8g protein; 10.9g fibre
suitable to freeze at the end of step 2.

spicy lentil soup

Accompaniments
POTATOES

prep + cook time 1¼ hours **serves** 4

ROAST POTATOES

Preheat oven to 220°C/425°F. Lightly oil oven tray. Cut 6 medium potatoes in half horizontally. Boil, steam or microwave potatoes 5 minutes; drain. Pat dry; cool 10 minutes. Gently rake rounded sides with tines of fork; place, in single layer, cut-side down, on oven tray. Brush with 2 tablespoons light olive oil, season; roast, uncovered, in oven, about 50 minutes or until potatoes are browned and crisp.

nutritional count per serving 9.4g total fat (1.3g saturated fat); 1246kJ (298 cal); 42.6g carbohydrate; 7.8g protein; 5.2g fibre

prep + cook time 1½ hours **serves** 4

HASSELBACK POTATOES

Preheat oven to 180°C/350°F. Cut 6 medium potatoes in half horizontally; slice thinly, without cutting all the way through. Coat in combined 40g (1½ ounces) melted butter and 2 tablespoons olive oil; place, in baking dish. Roast, uncovered, 45 minutes, brushing with oil mixture. Roast a further 15 minutes, without brushing, or until potatoes are tender. Sprinkle combined ¼ cup stale breadcrumbs and ½ cup finely grated cheddar cheese over potatoes; roast about 10 minutes or until browned lightly.

nutritional count per serving 22.9g total fat (10g saturated fat); 1756kJ (420 cal); 40.2g carbohydrate; 11.3g protein; 4.7g fibre

prep + cook time 20 minutes **serves** 4

POTATO CRUSH

Boil, steam or microwave 1kg (2 pounds) baby new potatoes until tender; drain. Mash about half the potatoes with ½ cup sour cream and 40g (1½ ounces) softened butter in large bowl until smooth. Using back of a fork or potato masher, gently crush remaining potatoes until skins burst and flesh is just flattened; fold into mash mixture. Season to taste. Sprinkle with 2 tablespoons coarsely chopped fresh flat-leaf parsley.

nutritional count per serving 20.4g total fat (13.2g saturated fat); 1480kJ (354 cal); 33.7g carbohydrate; 6.8g protein; 5g fibre

prep + cook time 30 minutes **serves** 4

CHEESY MASH

Coarsely chop 1kg (2 pounds) potatoes; boil, steam or microwave until tender, drain. Mash potato with 1 cup finely grated parmesan cheese, ⅔ cup finely grated mozzarella cheese, 1 cup mascarpone cheese and ½ cup hot milk in large bowl. Season to taste.

nutritional count per serving
48.1g total fat (31.3g saturated fat); 2763kJ (661 cal); 35.4g carbohydrate; 20.7g protein; 4g fibre

prep + cook time 35 minutes **serves** 4

COLCANNON

Coarsely chop 1kg (2 pounds) potatoes; boil, steam or microwave until tender, drain. Mash potato with ⅓ cup hot pouring cream and 40g (1½ ounces) softened butter in medium bowl until smooth. Melt 40g (1½ ounces) butter in frying pan; cook 2 finely chopped brown onions and 1 crushed garlic clove, stirring, until onion softens. Add 350g (11 ounces) finely shredded cabbage; cook, stirring, about 2 minutes or until cabbage just wilts. Fold potato mixture into cabbage mixture. Season to taste.

nutritional count per serving 25.5g total fat (16.5g saturated fat); 1835kJ (439 cal); 39.9g carbohydrate; 8.9g protein; 8.3g fibre

prep + cook time 1¼ hours **serves** 6

POTATOES ANNA

Preheat oven to 240°C/475°F. Oil shallow 2-litre (8-cup) 26cm (10¼-inch) round baking dish. Slice 1.2kg (2½ pounds) potatoes into 2mm (⅛ inch) slices; pat dry. Melt 100g (3 ounces) butter. Place a single layer of potato, slightly overlapping, into dish; brush with a little of the butter. Layer with remaining potato and butter, cover dish with foil; bake 20 minutes. Remove foil; Press down with metal spatula on potato. Reduce oven to 220°C/425°F; bake, uncovered, about 30 minutes or until top is crisp and browned lightly.

nutritional count per serving 13.9g total fat (9g saturated fat); 1066kJ (255 cal); 26.3g carbohydrate; 4.9g protein; 3.2g fibre

Fast forward

Don't think for a minute that a slow cooker must be used for hours and hours; it's also great for cooking food that needs shorter cooking times. In this chapter, we've tested recipes that cook to perfection in around four hours; very handy when you just can't wait to eat.

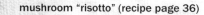

mushroom "risotto" (recipe page 36)

Heat butter in a large shallow frying pan, add onion; cook, stirring constantly, for about 5 minutes or until onion is soft.

Add wine; bring mixture to the boil, then reduce the heat and simmer until almost all of the liquid is evaporated.

Gradually stir in stock, the water and porcini mushrooms. Stir until mixture comes to the boil.

prep + cook time 2 hours 40 minutes **serves** 4

mushroom "risotto"

nutritional count per serving
26.6g total fat (16.6g saturated fat);
2947kJ (705 cal); 88.7g carbohydrate;
20g protein; 4.7g fibre
not suitable to freeze

(photograph page 35)

30g (1 ounce) butter
1 large brown onion (200g), chopped finely
½ cup (125ml) dry white wine
1 litre (4 cups) vegetable stock
2 cups (500ml) water
10g (½ ounce) dried porcini mushroom
  slices, torn
2 cups (400g) arborio rice

60g (2 ounces) butter, extra
300g (9½ ounces) button mushrooms,
  sliced thinly
200g (6½ ounces) swiss brown mushrooms,
  sliced thinly
2 cloves garlic, crushed
2 teaspoons finely chopped fresh thyme
1 cup (80g) finely grated parmesan cheese

Place rice in cooker, then pour in the onion mixture. Stir the ingredients until they are combined thoroughly.

Heat the butter in the pan; stir button mushrooms until browned, then remove from pan. Repeat step with the swiss brown mushrooms.

Stir button mushrooms and the swiss brown mushroom mixture into the cooker. Cook, uncovered, about 20 minutes, or until rice is tender.

This risotto has the texture of an oven-baked version rather than the creaminess of a traditional stirred risotto; it must be served immediately.

1 Heat butter in large frying pan; cook onion, stirring, until softened. Add wine; bring to the boil. Boil, uncovered, until liquid is almost evaporated. Add stock, the water and porcini; bring to the boil.
2 Place rice in 4.5-litre (18-cup) slow cooker; stir in onion mixture. Cook, covered, on high, 1½ hours. Stir well.
3 Meanwhile, heat 20g (¾ ounce) of the extra butter in same pan; cook button mushrooms, stirring occasionally, until browned. Remove from pan. Heat another 20g (¾ ounce) butter in same pan; cook swiss brown mushrooms, stirring occasionally, until browned. Add garlic and thyme; cook, stirring, until fragrant.
4 Stir button mushrooms and swiss brown mushroom mixture into cooker. Cook, uncovered, on high, about 20 minutes or until rice is tender.
5 Stir in cheese and remaining butter; season to taste. Serve immediately, sprinkled with extra thyme and parmesan cheese.

prep + cook time 4 hours 45 minutes **serves** 6

green chicken curry

nutritional count per serving
29.2g total fat (16.4g saturated fat);
1981kJ (474 cal); 16.2g carbohydrate;
35.4g protein; 4.7g fibre
tip Add curry paste to suit your heat level
tolerance; the strength of the paste will
differ between brands.
serving suggestion Serve with steamed
jasmine rice and lime wedges.
suitable to freeze at the end of step 1.

1kg (2 pounds) chicken thigh fillets, halved
2 cloves garlic, crushed
2.5cm (1-inch) piece fresh ginger (15g), grated
1 fresh long green chilli, chopped finely
2 tablespoons green curry paste
2 fresh kaffir lime leaves, torn
230g (7 ounces) canned sliced bamboo shoots, rinsed, drained
400g (12½ ounces) canned baby corn, rinsed, drained, chopped coarsely

¾ cup (180ml) chicken stock
1⅔ cup (410ml) coconut milk
2 tablespoons cornflour (cornstarch)
1 tablespoon water
1 tablespoon grated palm sugar
1 tablespoon lime juice
1 tablespoon fish sauce
⅔ cup loosely packed fresh thai basil leaves
⅓ cup loosely packed fresh coriander leaves (cilantro)

1 Combine chicken, garlic, ginger, chilli, paste, lime leaves, bamboo shoots, corn, stock and coconut milk in 4.5-litre (18-cup) slow cooker. Cook, covered, on low, 4 hours.
2 Blend cornflour with the water in small bowl until smooth. Stir cornflour mixture, sugar, juice, sauce and half the basil into cooker. Cook, uncovered, on high, about 20 minutes or until thickened slightly. Season to taste. Serve sprinkled with coriander and remaining basil.

prep + cook time 4 hours 30 minutes serves 8

panang lamb curry

nutritional count per serving
37.1g total fat (20.2g saturated fat);
2347kJ (501 cal); 13.47g carbohydrate;
42.3g protein; 3.7g fibre
tips Panang curry has a distinct peanut
flavour; the addition of peanut butter
helps to bring out the flavour when using
a bought paste. To reduce the fat content
of this recipe, use coconut milk or light
coconut milk.
not suitable to freeze

1 tablespoon peanut oil
1.5kg (3 pounds) boneless lamb shoulder,
 cut into 5cm (2-inch) pieces
½ cup (150g) panang curry paste
2½ cups (625ml) coconut cream
2 tablespoons fish sauce
¼ cup (65g) grated palm sugar
2 tablespoons peanut butter

4 fresh kaffir lime leaves
225g (7 ounces) canned sliced bamboo
 shoots, rinsed, drained
1 small red capsicum (bell pepper) (150g),
 sliced thinly
200g (6½ ounces) green beans, trimmed,
 halved
½ cup loosely packed fresh coriander
 leaves (cilantro)

1 Heat oil in large frying pan; cook lamb, in batches, until browned. Transfer to
   4.5-litre (18-cup) slow cooker.
2 Add paste to same pan; cook, stirring, about 1 minute or until fragrant. Add
   coconut cream, sauce, sugar, peanut butter and lime leaves; bring to the boil.
   Transfer to cooker.
3 Cook, covered, on low, 3½ hours. Add bamboo shoots, capsicum and beans to
   cooker; cook, covered, on low, about 30 minutes or until vegetables are tender.
   Season to taste.
4 Serve curry sprinkled with coriander.

prep + cook time 4 hours (+ refrigeration)
serves 6

pork and veal meatballs

1kg (2 pounds) minced (ground) pork and veal

1 cup (70g) stale breadcrumbs

1 cup (120g) finely grated cheddar cheese

2 eggs

1 cup finely chopped fresh flat-leaf parsley

4 cloves garlic, crushed

3½ cups (900g) bottled tomato pasta sauce (passata)

1 medium fennel bulb (300g), trimmed, sliced thinly

2 medium brown onions (300g), chopped finely

1 cup (80g) flaked parmesan cheese

1 Combine mince, breadcrumbs, cheddar, eggs, parsley and half the garlic in large bowl, season. Roll rounded tablespoons of mixture into balls. Place on tray, cover; refrigerate 20 minutes.

2 Combine sauce, fennel, onion and remaining garlic in 4.5-litre (18-cup) slow cooker; add meatballs. Cook, covered, on high, 3½ hours. Season to taste.

3 Serve sprinkled with parmesan.

nutritional count per serving 25.2g total fat (12.2g saturated fat); 2220kJ (531 cal); 20.3g carbohydrate; 52.4g protein; 6.1g fibre

tip Some butchers sell a pork and veal mince mixture, which is what we call for here. If it is not available as a mixture, buy half the amount in pork mince (500g/1 pound) and half the amount (500g/1 pound) as veal mince.

serving suggestions Serve the meatballs and sauce with spaghetti, soft polenta, couscous or simply with some crusty bread to mop up the sauce.

suitable to freeze at the end of step 2.

prep + cook time 4 hours 20 minutes
serves 8

octopus with chilli rice

1 Combine tomatoes, onion, garlic, bay leaf and the water in 4.5-litre (18-cup) slow cooker; add octopus, season. Cook, covered, on high, 3½ hours.
2 Carefully remove octopus from cooker to board. Stir rice into cooker; cook, covered, on high, 30 minutes.
3 When octopus is cool enough to handle, discard black skin; cut octopus into large chunks. Return octopus to cooker for remaining cooking time of rice.
4 Serve octopus and rice sprinkled with coriander and chilli.

nutritional count per serving 3.9g total fat (0.8g saturated fat); 1685kJ (403 cal); 37.8g carbohydrate; 51.8g protein; 2.7g fibre
tip Ask the fishmonger to clean the octopus for you.
not suitable to freeze

800g (1½ pounds) canned diced tomatoes
2 large brown onions (400g), chopped finely
6 cloves garlic, sliced thinly
1 dried bay leaf
1 litre (4 cups) water
1.5kg (3 pounds) large octopus, cleaned
1½ cups (300g) jasmine rice
1 cup coarsely chopped fresh coriander (cilantro)
2 fresh long red chillies, chopped finely

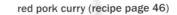
red pork curry (recipe page 46)

prep + cook time 4 hours 40 minutes **serves** 8

red pork curry

(photograph page 45)

. . . .

1⅔ cups (400ml) coconut cream

1 cup (250ml) salt-reduced chicken stock

¼ cup (75g) red curry paste

2 tablespoons fish sauce

3 fresh kaffir lime leaves, shredded finely

1.5kg (3 pounds) rindless boneless pork belly, chopped coarsely

2 large kumara (orange sweet potatoes) (1kg), chopped coarsely

500g (1 pound) snake beans, chopped coarsely

1 cup loosely packed fresh thai basil leaves

2 fresh long red chillies, sliced thinly

1 fresh kaffir lime leaf, shredded finely, extra

1 Combine coconut cream, stock, paste, sauce and lime leaves in 4.5-litre (18-cup) slow cooker; add pork and kumara. Cook, covered, on high, 4 hours.

2 Skim fat from surface. Stir in beans; cook, covered, on high, 30 minutes. Season to taste.

3 Serve sprinkled with basil, chilli and shredded lime leaf.

nutritional count per serving 21.9g total fat (12.1g saturated fat); 1831kJ (438 cal); 18.9g carbohydrate; 39.2g protein; 5.1g fibre
tip Ask the butcher to chop the pork belly for you.
serving suggestion Serve with steamed rice.
suitable to freeze at the end of step 2.

prep + cook time 4 hours 30 minutes (+ refrigeration) **serves** 4

barbecued american-style pork ribs

. . . .

2kg (4 pounds) american-style pork ribs

½ cup (140g) barbecue sauce

½ cup (140g) tomato sauce (ketchup)

½ cup (125ml) cider vinegar

¼ cup (85g) orange marmalade

3 cloves garlic, crushed

½ teaspoon chilli flakes

1 Cut pork into pieces to fit into cooker. Combine remaining ingredients in large shallow dish; add pork, turn to coat in marinade. Cover; refrigerate mixture overnight.

2 Transfer pork and marinade to 4.5-litre (18-cup) slow cooker; cook, covered, on high, 4 hours. Turn ribs twice during cooking time for even cooking.

3 Carefully remove ribs from cooker; cover to keep warm. Transfer sauce to large frying pan; bring to the boil. Reduce heat; simmer, uncovered, skimming fat from surface, for about 10 minutes or until sauce has reduced to about 1¾ cups. Serve pork drizzled with sauce.

nutritional count per serving 10.6g total fat (3.8g saturated fat); 1860kJ (445 cal); 38.2g carbohydrate; 48.6g protein; 1.7g fibre
tip Get your butcher to cut the ribs so that they will fit into your slow cooker.
serving suggestion Serve with steamed rice and lime wedges.
suitable to freeze at the end of step 3.

barbecued american-style pork ribs

prep + cook time 4 hours serves 6

chicken, celeriac and broad bean casserole

nutritional count per serving
33.4g total fat (8.6g saturated fat);
2504kJ (599 cal); 16.3g carbohydrate;
54.6g protein; 9.8g fibre
tip Roast the walnuts, in a preheated
180°C/350°F oven, for about 5 minutes
or until browned lightly.
suitable to freeze at the end of step 3.

1.5kg (3 pounds) chicken thigh fillets
2 tablespoons plain (all-purpose) flour
2 tablespoons vegetable oil
20g (¾ ounce) butter
1 large brown onion (200g), chopped
  coarsely
2 medium carrots (240g), sliced thickly
2 stalks celery (300g), trimmed,
  chopped coarsely

2 cloves garlic, chopped finely
2 cups (500ml) chicken stock
2 tablespoons dijon mustard
1 medium celeriac (celery root) (750g),
  chopped coarsely
2 cups (300g) frozen broad beans
  (fava beans)
½ cup (50g) walnuts, roasted,
  chopped coarsely
¼ cup coarsely chopped pale celery leaves

1 Toss chicken in flour to coat, shake off excess. Reserve excess flour. Heat oil in large frying pan; cook chicken, in batches, until browned. Remove from pan. Wipe pan with absorbent paper.
2 Heat butter in same pan; cook onion, carrot and celery, stirring, until softened. Add garlic; cook, stirring, until fragrant. Stir in reserved excess flour, then stock and mustard; stir over high heat until mixture boils and thickens.
3 Place celeriac in 4.5-litre (18-cup) slow cooker. Top with chicken then onion mixture. Cook, covered, on high, 3 hours.
4 Meanwhile, place broad beans in medium heatproof bowl, cover with boiling water; stand 2 minutes, drain. Peel away grey skins.
5 Add broad beans to cooker; cook, covered, on high, 30 minutes. Season to taste.
6 Serve sprinkled with nuts and celery leaves.

prep + cook time 4 hours 30 minutes **serves** 6

spinach and ricotta lasagne

nutritional count per serving
31.9g total fat (15.8g saturated fat);
2211kJ (529 cal); 25.1g carbohydrate;
32.7g protein; 8.3g fibre
serving suggestion Serve with a rocket
salad, and some crusty bread.
suitable to freeze at the end of step 3.

500g (1 pound) frozen spinach, thawed
3 cups (720g) ricotta cheese
2 eggs
1 cup (80g) finely grated parmesan cheese
cooking-oil spray
750g (1½ pounds) bottled tomato pasta
   sauce (passata)
⅓ cup (90g) basil pesto
6 dried instant lasagne sheets
1 cup (100g) coarsely grated mozzarella
   cheese

1 Squeeze excess moisture from spinach; place spinach in large bowl. Add
ricotta, eggs and half the parmesan; mix well, season.
2 Spray the bowl of 4.5-litre (18-cup) slow cooker lightly with cooking oil.
Combine sauce and pesto in medium bowl, season; spread ½ cup of the
sauce mixture over base of cooker.
3 Place 2 lasagne sheets in cooker, breaking to fit. Spread one-third of the spinach
mixture over pasta; top with one-third of the sauce, then 2 more lasagne
sheets. Repeat layering, finishing with sauce. Sprinkle with mozzarella and
remaining parmesan. Cook, covered, on low, 4 hours or until pasta is tender.

prep + cook time 4 hours 20 minutes
serves 6

portuguese caldeirada

2 tablespoons olive oil

2 large brown onions (400g), sliced thickly

3 medium red capsicums (bell peppers) (600g), sliced thickly

1kg (2 pounds) potatoes, sliced thickly

1 cup (250ml) dry white wine

½ cup (125ml) water

800g (1½ pounds) thick white fish fillets, chopped coarsely

2 tablespoons olive oil, extra

1　Pour olive oil into 4.5-litre (18-cup) slow cooker; layer onion, capsicum and potato in cooker, seasoning between each layer. Add wine and the water. Cook vegetable mixture, covered, on high, 3½ hours.

2　Add fish to cooker, season; spoon vegetable mixture over fish. Cook, covered, on high, 30 minutes.

3　Serve drizzled with extra oil.

nutritional count per serving 15.4g total fat (2.6g saturated fat); 1689kJ (404 cal); 24.6g carbohydrate; 32.7g protein; 3.9g fibre

tip You can use any firm white fish you like; choose large pieces. We used a mixture of angel and monk fish.

serving suggestion Serve with crusty bread.

not suitable to freeze

Caldeirada is a Portuguese fish stew. It varies from region to region, but usually contains a variety of fish, and occasionally shellfish, along with potato, onion and tomato, or capsicum, as we use here. It is similar to the French seafood stew, bouillabaisse.

prep + cook time 4 hours 30 minutes
serves 4

jerk-spiced chicken drumsticks

1 Heat half the oil in large frying pan; cook chicken, turning, until browned all over. Place chicken in 4.5-litre (18-cup) slow cooker.
2 Meanwhile, process onion, ginger, spices, chilli, pepper, garlic, thyme and remaining oil until finely chopped. Add sugar, vinegar and juice; process until smooth. Pour paste over chicken. Cook, covered, on low, 4 hours. Season to taste.
3 Serve chicken with sauce; sprinkle with extra thyme.

nutritional count per serving 30.1g total fat (7.6g saturated fat); 1831kJ (438 cal); 8.2g carbohydrate; 33.9g protein; 0.9g fibre
serving suggestion Serve with steamed green beans, rice and lime wedges.
suitable to freeze at the end of step 2.

2 tablespoons olive oil
8 chicken drumsticks (1.2kg)
4 green onions (scallions), chopped coarsely
5cm (2-inch) piece fresh ginger (20g), grated
1½ teaspoons ground allspice
½ teaspoon ground cinnamon
2 fresh long green chillies, chopped coarsely
1 teaspoon cracked black pepper
2 cloves garlic, crushed
3 teaspoons finely chopped fresh thyme
2 tablespoons light brown sugar
1 tablespoon cider vinegar
2 tablespoons orange juice

balti lamb and
rice meatballs
(recipe page 56)

prep + cook time 4 hours 30 minutes (+ refrigeration) **serves** 6

balti lamb and rice meatballs

(photograph page 55)

750g (1½ pounds) minced (ground) lamb
¾ cup (150g) uncooked jasmine rice
1 cup (70g) stale breadcrumbs
1 egg
2 tablespoons finely chopped fresh
   coriander (cilantro)
½ cup (150g) balti curry paste
2½ cups (625ml) water
400g (12½ ounces) canned diced
   tomatoes
2 medium brown onions (300g),
   chopped finely
650g (1¼ pounds) baby eggplant, halved
   lengthways, chopped coarsely
½ cup loosely packed fresh coriander
   leaves (cilantro), extra

1 Combine lamb, rice, breadcrumbs, egg and coriander in large bowl, season; roll level tablespoons of mixture into balls. Place on tray, cover; refrigerate 20 minutes.

2 Combine paste and the water in large jug; pour into 4.5-litre (18-cup) slow cooker. Stir in undrained tomatoes and onion; add meatballs and eggplant. Cook, covered, on high, 4 hours. Season to taste.

3 Serve sprinkled with extra coriander.

nutritional count per serving 19g total fat (5.4g saturated fat); 1969kJ (471 cal); 37.5g carbohydrate; 33.7g protein; 7.3g fibre
tip Make sure the meatballs are completely submerged in the liquid during cooking.
suitable to freeze at the end of step 2.

prep + cook time 4 hours 15 minutes **serves** 6

chicken tikka masala

1kg (2 pounds) skinless chicken thigh
   cutlets
800g (1½ pounds) canned diced tomatoes
2 large brown onions (400g), sliced thinly
⅔ cup (200g) tikka masala paste
¼ cup (60ml) pouring cream
1 cup loosely packed fresh coriander
   leaves (cilantro)

1 Combine chicken, undrained tomatoes, onion and paste in 4.5-litre (18-cup) slow cooker; cook, covered, on high, 4 hours. Season to taste.

2 Drizzle with cream, sprinkle with coriander.

nutritional count per serving 22.3g total fat (5.9g saturated fat); 1467kJ (351 cal); 10.8g carbohydrate; 24.2g protein; 6g fibre
serving suggestions Serve with steamed rice, naan bread and raita (a minted yogurt and cucumber dish).
suitable to freeze at the end of step 1.

chicken tikka masala

prep + cook time 3 hours serves 4

okra curry

nutritional count per serving
46.8g total fat (30.9g saturated fat);
2395kJ (573 cal); 17.4g carbohydrate;
14g protein; 16.9g fibre
tip This recipe serves 4 as a vegetarian
main meal with rice, but you can also
serve it as part of an Indian banquet to
serve 8.
serving suggestions Serve with steamed
rice and lime wedges.
suitable to freeze at the end of step 2.

¼ cup (60ml) peanut oil
2 large brown onions (400g), sliced thinly
2 fresh long green chillies, quartered
   lengthways
4cm (1½-inch) piece fresh ginger (20g),
   grated
5 cloves garlic, crushed
2 teaspoons ground coriander

1 teaspoon garam masala
½ teaspoon each ground turmeric and
   chilli powder
2 medium tomatoes (300g), chopped
   coarsely
1kg (2 pounds) okra, trimmed
2½ cups (625ml) coconut milk

Okra, also known as
lady fingers, is a green,
ridged, oblong pod with
a furry skin. While native
to Africa, this vegetable
is used in Indian, Middle-
Eastern and southern US
cooking. It often serves
as a thickener in stews.

1 Heat oil in large saucepan; cook onion, stirring, until soft and browned lightly.
   Add chilli, ginger and garlic; cook, stirring, until fragrant. Stir in spices; cook,
   stirring, 1 minute. Add tomato; cook, stirring, 2 minutes.
2 Transfer tomato mixture to 4.5-litre (18-cup) slow cooker with okra and
   coconut milk; season. Cook, covered, on high, 2½ hours.

Accompaniments
VEGETABLE MASHES

prep + cook time 30 minutes **serves** 4

KUMARA MASH

Coarsely chop 500g (1 pound) kumara (orange sweet potato) and 500g (1 pound) potatoes; boil, steam or microwave together, until tender; drain. Mash in large bowl; stir in ¼ cup hot chicken stock and 40g (1½ ounces) melted butter. Season to taste.

nutritional count per serving
8.5g total fat (5.4g saturated fat); 1024kJ (245 cal); 34.2g carbohydrate; 5.6g protein; 4.3g fibre

prep + cook time 30 minutes **serves** 4

CAPSICUM MASH

Quarter 2 red capsicums (bell peppers); discard seeds and membranes. Roast under hot grill, skin-side up, until skin blisters and blackens. Cover capsicum with plastic or paper for 5 minutes, then peel away skin; chop capsicum coarsely. Blend capsicum until smooth. Meanwhile, boil, steam or microwave 1kg (2 pounds) coarsely chopped potato until tender, drain. Mash potato in large bowl; stir in ½ cup hot pouring cream and 20g (¾ ounce) softened butter. Add capsicum to mash; stir until combined. Season to taste.

nutritional count per serving 18g total fat (11.6g saturated fat); 1446kJ (346 cal); 36.2g carbohydrate; 7.7g protein; 4.7g fibre

prep + cook time 30 minutes **serves** 4

FENNEL MASH

Slice 1 large fennel bulb thinly. Melt 60g (2 ounces) butter in large frying pan; cook fennel, covered, over low heat, about 10 minutes or until fennel is very soft. Blend or process fennel until smooth. Meanwhile, boil, steam or microwave 1kg (2 pounds) coarsely chopped potato until tender; drain. Mash potato in large bowl; stir in fennel mixture and ½ cup hot pouring cream. Season to taste.

nutritional count per serving 13.8g total fat (8.9g saturated fat); 1296kJ (310 cal); 36g carbohydrate; 7.3g protein; 6.1g fibre

prep + cook time **30** minutes **serves 4**

PEA MASH

Coarsely chop 1kg (2 pounds) potatoes; boil, steam or microwave potato and 1½ cups frozen peas, separately, until tender; drain. Mash potato in large bowl; stir in ¾ cup hot milk and 50g (1½ ounces) softened butter. Using fork, mash peas in small bowl; stir into potato mixture. Season to taste.

nutritional count per serving 12.6g total fat (8g saturated fat); 1392kJ (333 cal); 39.8g carbohydrate; 11.1g protein; 7.5g fibre

prep + cook time **30** minutes **serves 4**

SPINACH MASH

Coarsely chop 1kg (2 pounds) potatoes; boil, steam or microwave until tender, drain. Meanwhile, boil, steam or microwave 220g (7 ounces) trimmed spinach leaves until wilted; drain. When cool enough to handle, squeeze out excess liquid. Blend or process spinach with 40g (1½ ounces) softened butter until almost smooth. Mash potato in large bowl; stir in ½ cup hot pouring cream and spinach mixture. Season to taste.

nutritional count per serving 22.1g total fat (14.3g saturated fat); 1576kJ (377 cal); 34g carbohydrate; 8g protein; 5.5g fibre

prep + cook time **30** minutes **serves 4**

POTATO AND CELERIAC MASH

Coarsely chop 800g (1½ pounds) potatoes and 1kg (2 pounds) celeriac; boil, steam or microwave potato and celeriac, separately, until tender; drain. Mash potato and celeriac in large bowl; stir in ½ cup hot pouring cream and 60g (2 ounces) softened butter. Season to taste.

nutritional count per serving 26.5g total fat (17g saturated fat); 1835kJ (439 cal); 39.7g carbohydrate; 5.5g protein; 10.7g fibre

slow cooker
Prepare ahead

This chapter is for the organised person who is prepared to do a little work beforehand. These recipes, most of which are cooked in six to eight hours, need some browning, or some part cooked before the slow cooking is ready to start.

lamb biryani-style (recipe page 64)

Heat half the ghee in large frying pan, add nuts; stir constantly over heat until nuts are browned all over, then remove from pan.

Heat the remaining ghee in the frying pan, add onion; cook, stirring over heat, about 10 minutes, or until the onion is soft and browned lightly.

Heat the oil in the same frying pan; cook the lamb, in batches, stirring, until the lamb is browned evenly all over.

prep + cook time 9 hours **serves** 8

lamb biryani-style

nutritional count per serving
24.2g total fat (11.2g saturated fat);
2307kJ (552 cal); 45.2g carbohydrate;
36.8g protein; 2.1g fibre
serving suggestion Serve with raita.
not suitable to freeze

(photograph page 63)

40g (1½ ounces) ghee
½ cup (40g) flaked almonds
2 large brown onions (400g), sliced thinly
1 tablespoon vegetable oil
1.2kg (2½ pounds) boneless lamb shoulder, chopped coarsely
20g (¾ ounce) ghee, extra
4 cloves garlic, crushed
5cm (2-inch) piece fresh ginger (25g), grated
2 fresh long green chillies, sliced thinly
2 teaspoons each ground cumin and coriander

3 teaspoons garam masala
¾ cup (200g) greek-style yogurt
½ cup coarsely chopped fresh coriander (cilantro)
¼ cup coarsely chopped fresh mint
1 litre (4 cups) water
pinch saffron threads
2 tablespoons hot milk
2 cups (400g) basmati rice
1 lime, cut into wedges
½ cup loosely packed fresh coriander leaves (cilantro)

Heat the extra ghee in the frying pan; cook aromatics, then stir into the cooker with the other ingredients. Stir in half the water.

Heat the milk in a small microwave-safe bowl, sprinkle the saffron threads over the hot milk; stand 15 minutes.

Spoon cooked rice over cooked lamb mixture; drizzle with milk mixture, then top with onion mixture and nuts.

Biryani is a rice-based dish made with spices and meat, chicken, fish or vegetables. There are many versions available as this delicious recipe is a favourite across the Middle-East and India.

1 Heat half the ghee in large frying pan; cook nuts, stirring, until browned lightly. Remove from pan. Heat remaining ghee in same pan; cook onion, stirring, about 10 minutes or until soft and browned lightly. Remove from pan.

2 Heat oil in same pan; cook lamb, in batches, until browned. Transfer to 4.5-litre (18-cup) slow cooker. Heat extra ghee in same pan; cook garlic, ginger, chilli and spices, stirring, until fragrant. Remove from heat; stir in yogurt, chopped herbs and half the onion mixture. Transfer to cooker with half the water. Cook, covered, on low, 8 hours. Season to taste.

3 Meanwhile, sprinkle saffron over hot milk in small bowl; stand 15 minutes. Wash rice under cold water until water runs clear; drain. Combine rice and the remaining water in medium saucepan, cover; bring to the boil. Reduce heat; simmer, covered, about 8 minutes or until rice is tender. Season to taste.

4 Spoon rice over lamb in cooker; drizzle with milk mixture. Top with remaining onion mixture and nuts; cook, covered, about 30 minutes or until heated through.

5 Serve with lime wedges; sprinkle with coriander leaves.

prep + cook time 6 hours 35 minutes serves 6

meatballs in tomato sauce

nutritional count per serving
18.1g total fat (7.5g saturated fat);
1689kJ (404 cal); 18.4g carbohydrate;
39.7g protein; 4.4g fibre
serving suggestion Serve meatballs with spaghetti or mashed potato, sprinkle with parmesan cheese.
suitable to freeze at the end of step 2.

2 slices white bread (90g), crusts removed
½ cup (125ml) milk
1kg (2 pounds) minced (ground) beef
1 large brown onion (200g), chopped finely
1 medium carrot (120g), grated finely
3 cloves garlic, crushed
1 egg
2 tablespoons tomato paste
½ teaspoon dried oregano leaves
2 tablespoons finely chopped fresh basil
1 tablespoon olive oil

1 medium brown onion (150g), chopped finely, extra
2 cloves garlic, crushed, extra
400g (12½ ounces) canned diced tomatoes
400g (12½ ounces) canned cherry tomatoes
2 tablespoons tomato paste, extra
1 cup (250ml) beef stock
¼ cup loosely packed fresh basil leaves

1 Combine bread and milk in large bowl; stand 10 minutes. Add beef, onion, carrot, garlic, egg, paste, oregano and chopped basil, season; mix well. Shape level tablespoons of mixture into balls. Transfer to 4.5-litre (18-cup) slow cooker.
2 Heat oil in large frying pan; cook extra onion and garlic, stirring, until onion softens. Stir in undrained tomatoes, extra paste and stock; transfer to cooker. Cook, covered, on low, 6 hours. Season to taste.
3 Serve sprinkled with basil leaves.

prep + cook time 6 hours 20 minutes
serves 6

veal with balsamic sage sauce

6 pieces veal osso buco (1.2kg)
2 tablespoons plain (all-purpose) flour
1 tablespoon olive oil
20g (¾ ounce) butter
2 cloves garlic, sliced thinly
2 tablespoons coarsely chopped fresh sage
½ cup (125ml) balsamic vinegar
1 cup (250ml) chicken stock

1 Trim excess fat from veal; toss in flour to coat, shake off excess. Heat oil and butter in large frying pan; cook veal, in batches, until browned. Transfer to 4.5-litre (18-cup) slow cooker.

2 Add garlic and sage to same pan; cook, stirring, until fragrant. Add vinegar; boil, uncovered, about 2 minutes or until reduced by half. Stir in stock. Transfer to cooker.

3 Cook, covered, on low, 6 hours. Season to taste. Serve sprinkled with extra sage.

nutritional count per serving 9.8g total fat (3.7g saturated fat); 945kJ (226 cal); 3.4g carbohydrate; 30.1g protein; 0.3g fibre
tips Veal forequarter chops are also suitable for this recipe. Use regular balsamic vinegar, not an aged vinegar or glaze.
serving suggestions Serve with cheese risotto, soft polenta or mashed potato, and steamed green vegetables.
suitable to freeze at the end of step 3.

prep + cook time 6 hours 25 minutes
serves 4

spiced chicken with dates and chickpeas

1 Toss chicken in flour to coat, shake off excess. Heat half the oil in large frying pan; cook chicken, in batches, until browned. Remove from pan.

2 Heat remaining oil in same pan; cook onion, stirring, until onion softens. Add garlic, chilli and spices; cook, stirring, about 2 minutes or until fragrant. Stir in honey.

3 Place half the chicken in 4.5-litre (18-cup) slow cooker; top with half the spice mixture. Top with remaining chicken then remaining spice mixture. Pour stock over chicken. Cook, covered, on low, 5 hours.

4 Add chickpeas, zucchini and dates around the outside edge of cooker. Cook, covered, 1 hour. Stir in juice; season to taste. Serve sprinkled with coriander.

nutritional count per serving 31.3g total fat (7.8g saturated fat); 2926kJ (700 cal); 42.1g carbohydrate; 60.8g protein; 7.4g fibre
serving suggestions Serve with couscous or afghani (flat) bread.
suitable to freeze at the end of step 3.

8 skinless chicken thigh cutlets (1.6kg)
2 tablespoons plain (all-purpose) flour
2 tablespoons olive oil
2 medium brown onions (300g), cut into thin wedges
4 cloves garlic, chopped finely
1 fresh long red chilli, sliced thinly
2 teaspoons each ground cumin and cinnamon
¼ teaspoon saffron threads
2 tablespoons honey
2 cups (500ml) chicken stock
400g (12½ ounces) canned chickpeas (garbanzo beans), rinsed, drained
3 small zucchini (270g), sliced thickly
6 fresh dates (120g), halved, seeded
2 tablespoons lemon juice
⅓ cup loosely packed fresh coriander (cilantro) leaves

prep + cook time 7 hours **serves** 6

lamb chops with anchovies, chilli and cavolo nero

nutritional count per serving
20.1g total fat (5.4g saturated fat);
1387kJ (332 cal); 4.3g carbohydrate;
29.5g protein; 1.2g fibre
serving suggestion Serve with creamy
polenta, mashed potato or risotto.
suitable to freeze at the end of step 3.

1.5kg (3 pounds) lamb shoulder chops
2 tablespoons plain (all-purpose) flour
⅓ cup (80ml) olive oil
4 cloves garlic, sliced thinly
8 drained anchovy fillets, chopped finely
2 fresh long red chillies, sliced thinly
½ cup (125ml) dry white wine
1½ cups (375ml) chicken stock
100g (3 ounce) bunch cavolo nero
  (tuscan cabbage), chopped coarsely
½ cup coarsely chopped fresh flat-leaf
  parsley

Cavolo nero is a cabbage originally from Tuscany, Italy. It is available from some supermarkets and greengrocers. If it is unavailable, use silver beet (swiss chard) or spinach. Lamb forequarter chops can be used if you prefer.

1 Trim excess fat from lamb. Toss lamb in flour to coat, shake off excess. Reserve excess flour. Heat 1 tablespoon of the oil in large frying pan; cook lamb, in batches, until browned. Transfer to 4.5-litre (18-cup) slow cooker. Sprinkle reserved excess flour over lamb.

2 Wipe out pan with absorbent paper. Heat remaining oil in same pan; cook garlic, anchovy and chilli, stirring, until anchovies are soft. Add wine; bring to the boil. Boil, uncovered, until liquid is almost evaporated. Add stock; bring to the boil.

3 Transfer stock mixture to cooker. Cook, covered, on low, 6 hours.

4 Add cavolo nero; cook, covered, on low, about 30 minutes or until cavolo nero wilts. Season to taste. Stir in parsley.

prep + cook time 6 hours serves 6

braised beef with red wine and mushroom sauce

nutritional count per serving
30.9g total fat (13.4g saturated fat);
2316kJ (554 cal); 5.8g carbohydrate;
51.6g protein; 2.9g fibre
tip The piece of blade steak is also known
as a "bolar of blade", or just "bolar blade";
it is a shoulder cut. Beef silverside or rolled
brisket are also suitable to use.
serving suggestion Serve with spinach
mash and steamed green beans.
not suitable to freeze

2 tablespoons vegetable oil
1.3kg (2½-pound) piece beef blade
6 shallots (150g), chopped finely
1 stalk celery (150g), trimmed,
  chopped finely
1 medium carrot (120g), chopped finely
2 cloves garlic, crushed
2 sprigs fresh thyme
1½ cups (375ml) dry red wine

1 cup (250ml) beef stock
2 tablespoons plain (all-purpose) flour
2 tablespoons water
400g (12½ ounces) button mushrooms,
  halved
⅓ cup (80ml) pouring cream
2 teaspoons wholegrain mustard

1 Heat half the oil in large frying pan; cook beef, until browned all over. Transfer
  to 4.5-litre (18-cup) slow cooker.
2 Heat remaining oil in same pan; cook shallot, celery and carrot, stirring, until
  softened. Add garlic and thyme; cook, stirring, until fragrant. Add wine; bring
  to the boil. Boil, uncovered, until liquid is reduced by half. Transfer to cooker
  with stock; mix well.
3 Cook, covered, on low, 5 hours. Remove beef from cooker; cover with foil.
  Stand 15 minutes before slicing.
4 Meanwhile, strain liquid into large jug; discard solids. Blend flour with the
  water in small bowl until smooth. Return cooking liquid to cooker with flour
  mixture and mushrooms. Cook, uncovered, on high, about 30 minutes or until
  sauce thickens. Stir in cream and mustard; season to taste.
5 Serve sliced beef with sauce.

prep + cook time 3 hours serves 6

chana masala

2 large brown onions (400g), chopped coarsely

8 cloves garlic, quartered

6cm (2¼-inch) piece fresh ginger (60g), grated

2 tablespoons tomato paste

125g (4 ounces) ghee

2 teaspoons each ground coriander and garam masala

1 teaspoon ground turmeric

½ teaspoon ground chilli

800g (1½ pounds) canned chickpeas (garbanzo beans), rinsed, drained

1½ cups (375ml) water

½ cup loosely packed fresh coriander leaves (cilantro)

1 Blend onion, garlic, ginger and paste until smooth.

2 Heat ghee in large saucepan; cook onion mixture, stirring, 5 minutes. Add spices; cook, stirring, 2 minutes. Transfer to 4.5-litre (18-cup) slow cooker with chickpeas and the water. Cook, covered, on high, 2½ hours. Season to taste.

3 Serve sprinkled with coriander.

nutritional count per serving 22.1g total fat (13.4g saturated fat); 1283kJ (307 cal); 17.9g carbohydrate; 7.2g protein; 6.3g fibre
serving suggestions Serve with yogurt and naan (flat) bread.
suitable to freeze at the end of step 2.

Chana masala is a spicy vegetarian chickpea curry popular in Pakistan and India. It has a slightly sourish taste.

prep + cook time 8 hours 30 minutes
(+ refrigeration) **serves** 8

andalusian pork

1 Combine pork with spices, garlic, juice, bay leaves and half the oil in large bowl; turn to coat. Cover; refrigerate overnight.

2 Heat large frying pan; cook chorizo until browned. Transfer to 4.5-litre (18-cup) slow cooker; discard pan drippings.

3 Heat remaining oil in same pan; cook pork, in batches, until browned all over. Transfer to cooker; stir in onion, capsicum, stock and vinegar. Cook, covered, on slow, 8 hours. Skim fat from surface. Season to taste. Sprinkle with parsley.

nutritional count per serving 28.1g total fat (8.2g saturated fat); 1990kJ (476 cal); 6.7g carbohydrate; 48.3g protein; 1.7g fibre
tip You can quickly peel the capsicum with a vegetable peeler if you don't like the skin peeling off when it's cooked.
serving suggestions Serve with crusty bread and rice pilaf.
suitable to freeze at the end of step 3.

1.5kg (3 pounds) pork neck,
  chopped coarsely
1 tablespoon ground cumin
2 teaspoons each sweet smoked paprika
  and cayenne pepper
5 cloves garlic, crushed
2 tablespoons lemon juice
3 dried bay leaves
⅓ cup (80ml) olive oil
2 cured chorizo sausages (340g),
  sliced thinly
2 large brown onions (400g), sliced thinly
2 medium red capsicums (bell peppers)
  (400g), sliced thickly
1 cup (250ml) salt-reduced chicken stock
⅓ cup (80ml) sherry vinegar
⅓ cup coarsely chopped fresh
  flat-leaf parsley

prep + cook time 7 hours serves 6

lamb stew with artichokes and peas

nutritional count per serving
14g total fat (4.5g saturated fat);
1271kJ (304 cal); 8.9g carbohydrate;
30.1g protein; 4g fibre
tip Lamb forequarter and chump chops
are also suitable for this recipe.
suitable to freeze at the end of step 3.

1.5kg (3 pounds) lamb shoulder chops
2 tablespoons plain (all-purpose) flour
2 tablespoons olive oil
12 fresh sage leaves
1 large brown onion (200g),
 chopped coarsely
2 stalks celery (300g), trimmed,
 chopped coarsely
1 large carrot (180g), chopped coarsely

4 cloves garlic, chopped finely
½ cup (125ml) dry white wine
1½ cups (375ml) chicken stock
1 tablespoon coarsely chopped fresh sage
½ cup (60g) frozen peas
360g (11½ ounces) small fresh artichokes,
 trimmed, halved, centre chokes removed

1   Trim excess fat from lamb. Toss lamb in flour to coat, shake off excess. Reserve excess flour. Heat half the oil in large frying pan, cook sage leaves until browned lightly and crisp; drain on absorbent paper.
2   Cook lamb in same pan, in batches, until browned. Transfer to 4.5-litre (18-cup) slow cooker. Sprinkle reserved excess flour over lamb.
3   Heat remaining oil in same pan; cook onion, celery and carrot, stirring, until softened. Add garlic; cook, stirring, until fragrant. Add wine; bring to the boil. Boil, uncovered, until liquid is almost evaporated. Stir onion mixture, stock and extra sage into cooker. Cook, covered, on low, 6 hours.
4   Add peas and artichokes to cooker; cook, covered, 30 minutes. Season to taste. Serve sprinkled with crisp sage leaves.

prep + cook time 8 hours 30 minutes
serves 8

pork and green olive stew

2 tablespoons olive oil

1.5kg (3 pounds) pork neck, chopped
  coarsely

1¼ cups (310ml) salt-reduced chicken stock

¾ cup (180ml) dry white wine

1 large brown onion (200g), chopped finely

4 cloves garlic, crushed

1 tablespoon coarsely chopped fresh
  rosemary

1.5kg (3 pounds) kipfler (fingerling)
  potatoes, unpeeled, halved

½ cup (60g) seeded green olives

1 Heat oil in large frying pan; cook pork, in batches, until browned. Transfer to 4.5-litre (18-cup) slow cooker.

2 Add stock, wine, onion, garlic and rosemary to cooker; stir to combine. Top with potato. Cook, covered, on low, 8 hours. Skim fat from surface; stir in olives. Season to taste.

nutritional count per serving 10.9g total fat (3g saturated fat); 1731kJ (414 cal); 28.5g carbohydrate; 43.5g protein; 4.4g fibre
serving suggestion Serve with crusty bread to mop up the juices.
not suitable to freeze

prep + cook time 8 hours 45 minutes
serves 6

massaman beef curry

1 Heat half the oil in large frying pan; cook onion, stirring, about 10 minutes or until browned lightly. Transfer to 4.5-litre (18-cup) slow cooker.
2 Heat remaining oil in same pan; cook beef, in batches, until browned. Add paste; cook, stirring, 1 minute or until fragrant. Transfer to cooker.
3 Add coconut milk, stock, cinnamon, bay leaves, potato and nuts to cooker. Cook, covered, on low, 8 hours.
4 Stir in sugar and sauce. Serve sprinkled with coriander; accompany with lime wedges.

nutritional count per serving 48.3g total fat (16.6g saturated fat); 3051kJ (730 cal); 25.9g carbohydrate; 45.6g protein; 7.5g fibre
tip Chuck steak is also suitable for this recipe.
not suitable to freeze

2 tablespoons peanut oil
2 large brown onions (400g), cut into thin wedges
1kg (2 pounds) gravy beef, chopped coarsely
⅔ cup (200g) massaman curry paste
1 cup (250ml) coconut milk
1 cup (250ml) chicken stock
2 cinnamon sticks
2 dried bay leaves
3 medium potatoes (600g), chopped coarsely
½ cup (70g) roasted unsalted peanuts
2 tablespoons light brown sugar
1 tablespoons fish sauce
⅓ cup lightly packed fresh coriander leaves (cilantro)
1 lime, cut into wedges

prep + cook time 5 hours serves 4

chicken and chorizo paella

nutritional count per serving
21.6g total fat (6.2g saturated fat);
2320kJ (555 cal); 43.8g carbohydrate;
42.9g protein; 6.2g fibre
not suitable to freeze

1 tablespoon olive oil
500g (1 pound) chicken breast fillets,
   chopped coarsely
1 cured chorizo sausage (170g),
   sliced thinly
1 medium brown onion (150g),
   chopped finely
1 medium red capsicum (bell pepper)
   (200g), chopped finely
2 cloves garlic, crushed
½ teaspoon saffron threads
2 teaspoons smoked paprika

1 cup (250ml) chicken stock
400g (12½ ounces) canned diced tomatoes
500g (1 pound) packaged 90-second
   microwave white long grain rice
¾ cup (90g) frozen peas
½ cup (75g) pimiento-stuffed green olives,
   chopped coarsely
½ cup finely chopped fresh flat-leaf parsley

1 Heat oil in large frying pan; cook chicken and chorizo, in batches, until
   browned. Transfer to 4.5-litre (18-cup) slow cooker.
2 Add onion, capsicum, garlic, spices, stock and undrained tomatoes. Cook,
   covered, on low, 4 hours.
3 Stir in rice and peas. Cook, covered, on low, about 15 minutes or until hot.
   Season to taste. Serve sprinkled with olives and parsley.

prep + cook time 6 hours 40 minutes
serves 4

eggplant parmigiana

⅔ cup (160ml) olive oil

1 medium brown onion (150g),
  chopped finely

2 cloves garlic, crushed

400g (12½ ounces) canned diced tomatoes

1 cup (260g) bottled tomato pasta sauce
  (passata)

¼ teaspoon dried chilli flakes

2 medium eggplants (600g), sliced thickly

¼ cup (35g) plain (all-purpose) flour

⅓ cup loosely packed fresh basil leaves

200g (6½ ounces) bocconcini cheese,
  sliced thinly

⅔ cup (50g) finely grated parmesan cheese

½ teaspoon sweet paprika

1   Heat 1 tablespoon of the oil in large frying pan; cook onion, stirring, until onion softens. Add garlic; cook, stirring, until fragrant. Stir in undrained tomatoes, sauce and chilli. Transfer to medium jug.

2   Toss eggplant in flour to coat, dust off excess. Heat remaining oil in same pan; cook eggplant, in batches, until browned. Drain on absorbent paper.

3   Layer half the eggplant in 4.5-litre (18-cup) slow cooker; season. Top with half the tomato mixture, basil and bocconcini. Repeat layering, finishing with parmesan. Sprinkle with paprika. Cook, covered, on low, 6 hours.

nutritional count per serving 49.9g total fat (12.8g saturated fat); 2562kJ (613 cal); 20.6g carbohydrate; 18.5g protein; 7.2g fibre
serving suggestions Serve with crusty bread and rocket salad or stir through cooked short pasta.
not suitable to freeze

prep + cook time 4 hours 30 minutes
serves 4

creamy lemon thyme chicken

1 Heat half the oil in large frying pan; cook chicken, in batches, until browned. Transfer to 4.5-litre (18-cup) slow cooker.

2 Heat remaining oil in same pan; cook onion, stirring, about 10 minutes or until caramelised. Transfer to cooker with remaining ingredients. Cook, covered, on low, 4 hours. Discard thyme; season to taste.

nutritional count per serving 47g total fat (19.7g saturated fat); 3076kJ (736 cal); 20.5g carbohydrate; 51.8g protein; 4.9g fibre
serving suggestions Serve with mashed potato, cooked pasta or rice.
not suitable to freeze

2 tablespoons olive oil
1kg (2 pounds) chicken thigh fillets, halved
2 medium brown onions (300g), sliced thinly
1 medium fennel bulb (300g), sliced thinly
4 sprigs fresh lemon thyme
2 cloves garlic, crushed
½ cup (125ml) dry white wine
2 tablespoons wholegrain mustard
1 medium kumara (orange sweet potato) (400g), chopped coarsely
1 cup (250ml) chicken stock
¾ cup (180ml) pouring cream

prep + cook time 4 hours 40 minutes **serves** 4

cheat's chicken jambalaya

nutritional count per serving
16.9g total fat (5.7g saturated fat);
2562kJ (613 cal); 41.6g carbohydrate;
71.2g protein; 3.2g fibre
not suitable to freeze

500g (1 pound) chicken breast fillets, chopped coarsely

1 cured chorizo sausage (170g), sliced thinly

400g (12½ ounces) canned diced tomatoes

1 medium green capsicum (bell pepper) (200g), sliced thickly

1 medium red capsicum (bell pepper) (200g), sliced thickly

1 stalk celery (300g), trimmed, sliced thinly

1 cup (250ml) chicken stock

1 teaspoon dried oregano

1 tablespoon cajun seasoning

pinch cayenne pepper

2 dried bay leaves

500g (1 pound) cooked shelled prawns (shrimp)

500g (1 pound) packaged 90-second microwave white long-grain rice

Use fresh or frozen (thawed) prawns. Packets of frozen pre-cooked, shelled and deveined prawns are available from most large supermarkets or from fish markets.

1 Combine chicken, chorizo, undrained tomatoes, capsicum, celery, stock, oregano, seasoning, pepper and bay leaves in 4.5-litre (18-cup) slow cooker. Cook, covered, on low, 4 hours.

2 Stir in prawns and rice. Cook, covered, on low, about 15 minutes or until hot. Season to taste.

Accompaniments
RICE

prep + cook time 35 minutes **serves** 4

ALMOND PILAF

Melt 20g (¾ ounce) butter in medium saucepan; cook 1 crushed garlic clove, stirring, until fragrant. Add 1 cup basmati rice; cook, stirring, 1 minute. Add 1 cup chicken stock and 1 cup water; bring to the boil. Reduce heat; simmer, covered, about 20 minutes or until rice is tender. Remove from heat; fluff rice with fork. Stir in ¼ cup coarsely chopped fresh flat-leaf parsley and ¼ cup roasted flaked almonds. Season to taste.

nutritional count per serving
7.4g total fat (3.1g saturated fat); 1053kJ (252 cal); 40.3g carbohydrate; 5.2g protein; 1.2g fibre

prep + cook time 1 hour **serves** 6

RISOTTO MILANESE

Boil 3 cups chicken stock and pinch saffron threads in medium saucepan; simmer, covered. Heat 60g (2 ounces) butter in large pan; cook 1 finely chopped brown onion, stirring, until softened. Stir in 1¾ cups arborio rice. Stir in ½ cup dry white wine and 1 cup of the stock; bring to the boil. When liquid is almost absorbed, stir in another 1 cup of the stock; return to the boil. Repeat with remaining stock, then reduce heat. Cook until stock is absorbed and rice is tender. Stir in 2 tablespoons grated parmesan cheese. Season to taste.

nutritional count per serving 13.9g total fat (8.9g saturated fat); 1580kJ (378 cal); 52.2g carbohydrate; 7 protein; 0.9g fibre

prep + cook time 30 minutes (+ standing) **serves** 4

CLASSIC PULAO

Soak 1⅓ cups basmati rice in medium bowl of cold water for 20 minutes, drain. Melt 50g (1½ ounces) butter in large saucepan; stir in 1 finely chopped brown onion and 2 crushed garlic cloves until onion softens. Stir in 1 cinnamon stick and 1 dried bay leaf; cook 2 minutes. Add drained rice; cook, stirring, 2 minutes. Add 2½ cups hot chicken stock and ⅓ cup sultanas; simmer, covered, about 10 minutes or until rice is tender and liquid is absorbed. Sprinkle with ½ cup roasted unsalted cashews. Season to taste. Remove cinnamon before serving.

nutritional count per serving 20.6g total fat (8.8g saturated fat); 2128kJ (509 cal); 68.7g carbohydrate; 10.5g protein; 3g fibre

prep + cook time 30 minutes **serves** 6

SPANISH RICE AND PEAS

Combine 3 cups water and ¼ cup olive oil in medium saucepan; bring to the boil. Stir in 2 cups white medium-grain rice; cook, uncovered, without stirring, about 10 minutes or until liquid has almost evaporated. Reduce heat; simmer, covered, 5 minutes. Gently stir in 1 cup frozen peas; simmer, covered, about 5 minutes or until rice and peas are tender. Season to taste.

nutritional count per serving
9.5g total fat (1.4g saturated fat); 1379kJ (330 cal); 54.3g carbohydrate; 5.6g protein; 1.7g fibre

prep + cook time 15 minutes **serves** 8

WILD RICE SALAD WITH SPINACH AND FIGS

Cook 2 cups wild rice blend in large saucepan of boiling water until tender; drain. Rinse under cold water; drain. Place in large bowl. Meanwhile, place 2 teaspoons finely grated orange rind, ½ cup orange juice, 2 tablespoons olive oil and 1 tablespoon white balsamic vinegar in screw-top jar; shake well. Combine dressing, rice, ¾ cup coarsely chopped roasted pecans, ½ cup thinly sliced dried figs, 100g (3 ounces) baby spinach leaves and 2 thinly sliced green onions (scallions) in large bowl. Season to taste.

nutritional count per serving 13g total fat (1.2g saturated fat); 1359kJ (325 cal); 44.8g carbohydrate; 5.1g protein; 3.6g fibre

prep + cook time 20 minutes (+ standing) **serves** 4

YELLOW COCONUT RICE

Soak 1¾ cups white long-grain rice in large bowl of cold water 30 minutes. Rinse rice under cold water until water runs clear; drain. Place 1¼ cups water, 1⅔ cups coconut cream, 1 teaspoon white (granulated) sugar, ½ teaspoon ground turmeric, pinch saffron threads and rice in large heavy-based saucepan; cover pan, bring to the boil, stirring occasionally. Reduce heat; simmer, covered, without stirring, about 15 minutes or until rice is tender. Stand, covered, off the heat, 5 minutes. Season to taste.

nutritional count per serving 21.1g total fat (18.2g saturated fat); 2186kJ (523 cal); 73.9g carbohydrate; 7.7g protein; 2.4g fibre

slow cooker
Freezer friendly

All food will freeze, but it's how it looks and tastes when it's thawed and reheated that decides if a food is freezer friendly or not. Whole or large mushrooms and potato pieces, salad greens and hard-boiled eggs are to be avoided. For best results, thaw frozen food in the refrigerator overnight.

oxtail stew with red wine and port
(recipe page 90)

Trim as much fat as possible from the oxtail – it has a lot of hidden fat, which will need to be removed from the surface of the stew later.

Toss each piece of oxtail in a bowl of flour until it is coated evenly; shake off any excess flour.

Heat half the oil in a large frying pan, cook oxtail, in batches, until evenly browned all over; transfer to the cooker.

prep + cook time 9 hours 15 minutes **serves** 8

oxtail stew with red wine and port

nutritional count per serving
48.4g total fat (17.4g saturated fat); 2959kJ (708 cal); 14.5g carbohydrate; 30.9g protein; 2g fibre
serving suggestion Serve with potato, celeriac or parsnip puree.
suitable to freeze at the end of step 4. Pack oxtail into freezer-proof container; pour sauce over, leaving 2.5cm (1-inch) space to allow for expansion. Seal, label and freeze for up to 3 months.

(photograph page 89)

2kg (4 pounds) oxtails, cut into 5cm (2-inch) pieces
2 tablespoons plain (all-purpose) flour
2 tablespoons vegetable oil
12 brown pickling onions (480g)
2 medium carrots (240g), chopped coarsely
1 stalk celery (150g), trimmed, sliced thickly

8 cloves garlic, peeled
1½ cups (375ml) dry red wine
2 cups (500ml) port
2 cups (500ml) beef stock
4 sprigs fresh thyme
1 dried bay leaf

Cut the tops from the onions, then peel away the outer brown layer leaving the root ends intact. Trim the root ends neatly.

Heat the remaining oil in the same, cleaned, frying pan; cook the vegetables, in batches, stirring until lightly browned all over; add to the cooker.

Add the wine and port to the pan, bring to the boil; boil, uncovered until mixture reduces to about 1 cup.

Beef brisket, beef cheeks and chuck steak are all suitable to use in this recipe. Oxtails are often sold frozen or may need to be ordered from the butcher. The stew is best made a day ahead and refrigerated to set the fat, which can then be removed from the surface of the stew.

1 Trim excess fat from oxtail; toss oxtail in flour to coat, shake off excess Heat half the oil in large frying pan; cook oxtail, in batches, until browned. Transfer to 4.5-litre (18-cup) slow cooker.

2 Meanwhile, peel onions, leaving root ends intact.

3 Heat remaining oil in same pan; cook onions, carrot, celery and garlic, stirring, about 5 minutes or until vegetables are browned lightly. Transfer to cooker. Add wine and port to pan; bring to the boil. Boil, uncovered, until reduced to 1 cup. Transfer to cooker with stock, thyme and bay leaf. Cook, covered, on low, 8 hours.

4 Discard thyme and bay leaf. Remove oxtail from cooker; cover to keep warm. Cook sauce, uncovered, on high, about 30 minutes or until thickened. Skim fat from surface. Season to taste. Return oxtail to sauce to heat through.

prep + cook time 6 hours 30 minutes **serves** 8

mulligatawny soup with chicken

nutritional count per serving
28.5g total fat (16g saturated fat);
1981kJ (474 cal); 24.7g carbohydrate;
27.9g protein; 6.8g fibre
serving suggestion Serve with roti bread,
yogurt and lemon wedges.
suitable to freeze at the end of step 2.
Stir in coriander after reheating.
To freeze, pour soup into freezer-proof
containers, leaving 2.5cm (1-inch) space
to allow for expansion. Seal, label and
freeze for up to 3 months.

1 tablespoon vegetable oil
800g (1½ pounds) chicken thigh fillets,
    chopped coarsely
20g (¾ ounce) ghee
1 large brown onion (200g),
    chopped coarsely
2 stalks celery (300g), trimmed,
    chopped coarsely
2 medium carrots (240g), chopped coarsely
3 cloves garlic, chopped finely
¼ cup (75g) madras curry paste

2 medium potatoes (400g),
    chopped coarsely
1 medium kumara (orange sweet potato)
    (400g), chopped coarsely
½ cup (100g) dried red lentils, rinsed,
    drained
1.5 litres (6 cups) salt-reduced
    chicken stock
2 cups (500ml) coconut milk
¼ cup coarsely chopped fresh coriander
    (cilantro)
1 medium lemon (140g), cut into wedges

Mulligatawny is a
chicken soup flavoured
with Indian spices; it is a
product of the British Raj
in India. Mulligatawny
means 'pepper water',
and the Indians used to
drink it as a digestive.
Beef or lamb could be
used in this recipe,
instead of the chicken.

1 Heat oil in large frying pan; cook chicken, in batches, until browned. Transfer to 4.5-litre (18-cup) slow cooker.
2 Heat ghee in same pan; cook onion, celery and carrot, stirring, until onion softens. Add garlic and curry paste; cook, stirring, until fragrant. Transfer to cooker with potato, kumara, lentils, stock and coconut milk. Cook, covered, on low, 6 hours.
3 Stir in coriander; season to taste. Serve with lemon wedges.

prep + cook time 8 hours 15 minutes
makes 2.75 litres (11 cups)

vegetable stock

3 litres (12 cups) water

2 small leeks (400g), chopped coarsely

2 medium carrots (240g), unpeeled,
   chopped coarsely

1 large brown onion (200g), unpeeled,
   halved

2 stalks celery (300g), trimmed,
   chopped coarsely

1 medium tomato (150g), quartered

2 cloves garlic, unpeeled, bruised

1 teaspoon black peppercorns

1 teaspoon coarse cooking salt
   (kosher salt)

1 dried bay leaf

1 Combine ingredients in 4.5-litre (18-cup) slow cooker; cook, covered, on low, 8 hours. Stand 10 minutes; strain through muslin-lined sieve into large heatproof bowl. Discard solids.

nutritional count per 1 cup (250ml) 0.8g total fat (0.3g saturated fat); 125kJ (30 cal); 5.3g carbohydrate; 0.5g protein; 0g fibre
suitable to freeze Pour into 1-cup freezer-proof containers, leaving 2.5cm (1-inch) space to allow for expansion. Seal, label and freeze for up to 3 months.

prep + cook time 8 hours 30 minutes
makes 2 litres (8 cups)

chicken stock

1 Combine ingredients in 4.5-litre (18-cup) slow cooker; cook, covered, on low, 8 hours. Stand 10 minutes; strain through muslin-lined sieve into large heatproof bowl. Discard solids.
2 Refrigerate until fat sets; discard fat.

nutritional count per 1 cup (250ml) 1.9g total fat (0.6g saturated fat); 483kJ (105 cal); 4g carbohydrate; 16.8g protein; 1.8g fibre
tip Chicken shops often sell chicken carcasses – if not, chicken necks, with the skin removed, make excellent stock.
suitable to freeze Pour into 1-cup freezer-proof containers, leaving 2.5cm (1-inch) space to allow for expansion. Seal, label and freeze for up to 3 months.

2 litres (8 cups) water
600g (1¼ pounds) chicken carcasses
2 medium carrots (240g), unpeeled, halved
2 stalks celery stalks (300g) untrimmed, chopped coarsely
1 large brown onion (200g), unpeeled, quartered
1 dried bay leaf
1 teaspoon black peppercorns
1 teaspoon coarse cooking salt (kosher salt)

prep + cook time 6 hours 45 minutes serves 6

italian-style chilli beef

nutritional count per serving
14.2g total fat (5.2g saturated fat);
1329kJ (318 cal); 12.5g carbohydrate;
29.7g protein; 4.9g fibre
serving suggestions Serve with soft
polenta or crusty bread.
suitable to freeze at the end of step 3.
Pack into freezer-proof containers, leaving
2.5cm (1-inch) space to allow for expansion.
Seal, label and freeze for up to 3 months.
Stir in chopped basil after reheating.

1 tablespoon olive oil
750g (1½ pounds) lean minced
  (ground) beef
1 large brown onion (200g), chopped finely
3 cloves garlic, crushed
1 teaspoon dried chilli flakes
½ cup (125ml) dry red wine
½ cup (125ml) beef stock

2 medium red capsicums (bell peppers)
  (400g), chopped finely
500g (1 pound) bottled tomato pasta
  sauce (passata)
2 small zucchini (240g), chopped finely
400g (12½ ounces) canned cannellini
  beans, rinsed, drained
½ cup firmly packed fresh small
  basil leaves

1 Heat oil in large frying pan; cook beef and onion, stirring, until beef is browned.
   Add garlic and chilli; cook, stirring, about 1 minute or until fragrant. Add wine;
   bring to the boil. Boil, uncovered, about 1 minute or until liquid is almost
   evaporated. Transfer mince mixture to 4.5-litre (18-cup) slow cooker.
2 Stir in the stock, capsicum and sauce. Cook, covered, on low, 5 hours.
3 Stir in zucchini and beans. Cook, covered, on low, 1 hour.
4 Coarsely chop half the basil. Just before serving, stir in chopped basil; season
   to taste. Serve sprinkled with remaining basil.

prep + cook time 7 hours 25 minutes
(+ standing) **serves** 8

cauliflower soup

40g (1½ ounces) butter

2 large brown onions (400g),
  chopped coarsely

3 cloves garlic, crushed

1 litre (4 cups) vegetable stock

1.2kg (2½ pounds) cauliflower,
  cut into florets

2 medium potatoes (400g),
  chopped coarsely

2 cups (500ml) water

1¼ cups (310ml) pouring cream

2 tablespoons finely chopped fresh
  flat-leaf parsley

1 Heat butter in large frying pan; cook onion, stirring, until softened. Add garlic; cook, stirring, until fragrant. Add stock; bring to the boil.

2 Transfer onion mixture to 4.5-litre (18-cup) slow cooker with cauliflower, potato and the water. Cook, covered, on low, 6½ hours.

3 Blend or process soup, in batches, until smooth. Return to cooker; stir in cream. Cook, covered, on high, about 30 minutes or until soup is hot. Season to taste. Sprinkle with parsley.

nutritional count per serving 19.3g total fat (12.3g saturated fat); 1105kJ (264 cal); 114.9g carbohydrate; 6g protein; 4.1g fibre

tips It is fine just to use 1 x 300ml carton of cream for this recipe. You will need about 2 small cauliflowers for this recipe.

suitable to freeze Pour into freezer-proof containers, leaving 2.5cm (1-inch) space to allow for expansion. Seal, label and freeze for up to 3 months.

prep + cook time 4 hours 30 minutes
serves 8

petit salé aux lentilles

1 Heat oil in large frying pan; cook onion, stirring, until softened. Transfer to 4.5-litre (18-cup) slow cooker.

2 Cook sausages in same pan until browned; transfer to cooker with remaining ingredients. Cook, covered, on high, 4 hours. Season to taste.

nutritional count per serving 17.3g total fat (5.8g saturated fat); 2082kJ (498 cal); 32.3g carbohydrate; 49.5g protein; 11.7g fibre

tip Taste before adding any salt as the ham and sausages are quite salty. You can also use thick pork sausages.

suitable to freeze Shred meat from the ham bones and return to the lentil mixture. Pack into freezer-proof containers, leaving 2.5cm (1-inch) space to allow for expansion. Seal, label and freeze for up to 3 months.

1 tablespoon olive oil

2 large brown onions (400g), chopped finely

4 toulouse sausages 400g)

1.75 litres (7 cups) water

3 cups (600g) french-style green lentils

1.5kg (3 pounds) ham hock

5 cloves garlic, crushed

3 dried bay leaves

Meaning 'salted pork with lentils', in French, this hearty, rustic-style dish is a specialty of France's Auvergne region. Toulouse is a small French sausage made of coarsely diced pork and flavoured with wine, garlic and various seasonings. It is available from speciality butchers.

prep + cook time 4 hours 30 minutes serves 4

sweet and sour chicken

nutritional count per serving
16.1g total fat (4.6g saturated fat);
1986kJ (475 cal); 31.7g carbohydrate;
47.8g protein; 4.7g fibre
suitable to freeze at the end of step 2.
Pack into freezer-proof containers, leaving
2.5cm (1-inch) space to allow for expansion.
Seal, label and freeze for up to 3 months.
Sprinkle with green onion after reheating.

1 tablespoon vegetable oil
4 chicken lovely legs (520g)
4 skinless chicken thigh cutlets (800g)
2 medium red onions (340g), cut into
 wedges
½ cup (125ml) japanese soy sauce
½ cup (130g) bottled tomato pasta sauce
 (passata)
⅓ cup (80ml) pineapple juice
2 tablespoons firmly packed
 light brown sugar
2 tablespoons white vinegar

1 fresh long red chilli, chopped finely
2 cloves garlic, crushed
1 large red capsicum (bell pepper) (350g),
 chopped coarsely
1 large green capsicum (bell pepper)
 (350g), chopped coarsely
225g (7 ounces) canned pineapple pieces
 in juice
2 tablespoons cornflour (cornstarch)
2 tablespoons water
2 green onions (scallions), shredded finely

Use whatever cuts of chicken you like for this recipe – choose cuts on the bones for a moist result. Lovely legs are trimmed, skinless chicken drumsticks, available from supermarkets.

1 Heat oil in large frying pan; cook chicken, in batches, until browned. Transfer to 4.5-litre (18-cup) slow cooker. Add red onion, sauces, juice, sugar, vinegar, chilli, garlic, capsicum and undrained pineapple. Cook, covered, on low, 4 hours.
2 Blend cornflour with the water in small bowl until smooth. Add cornflour mixture to cooker. Cook, uncovered, on high, about 5 minutes or until thickened. Season to taste.
3 Serve sprinkled with green onion.

prep + cook time 6 hours 20 minutes
serves 6

lamb korma

1.5kg (3¼ pounds) boned lamb shoulder,
  chopped coarsely

2 medium brown onions (300g) sliced thinly

5cm (2-inch) piece fresh ginger (25g),
  grated

3 cloves garlic, crushed

⅔ cup (200g) korma paste

3 medium tomatoes (450g),
  chopped coarsely

½ cup (125ml) chicken stock

1¼ cups (310ml) pouring cream

1 cinnamon stick

2 teaspoons poppy seeds

½ cup loosely packed fresh coriander
  (cilantro) leaves

1 fresh long red chilli, sliced thinly

⅓ cup (25g) roasted flaked almonds

1 Combine lamb, onion, ginger, garlic, paste, tomatoes, stock, cream, cinnamon and seeds in 4.5-litre (18-cup) slow cooker. Cook, covered, on low, 6 hours. Season to taste.

2 Serve sprinkled with coriander, chilli and nuts.

nutritional count per serving 49.9g total fat (22.8g saturated fat); 3005kJ (719 cal); 9.3g carbohydrate; 55.7g protein; 6.2g fibre
serving suggestions Serve with steamed basmati rice, grilled naan (flat) bread and yogurt.
suitable to freeze at the end of step 1. Pack into freezer-proof containers, leaving 2.5cm (1-inch) space to allow for expansion. Seal, label and freeze for up to 3 months. Sprinkle with coriander, chilli and nuts after reheating.

prep + cook time 6 hours 30 minutes
serves 6

beef pot au feu

1 Peel onions, leaving root ends intact.
2 Rub beef all over with pepper. Place in 4.5-litre (18-cup) slow cooker. Add remaining ingredients. Cook, covered, on low, 6 hours. Season to taste.
3 Remove beef from cooker; shred into large pieces. Discard speck, herbs and bay leaves. Skim fat from surface of broth. Serve meat with vegetables and broth. Sprinkle with parsley before serving.

nutritional count per serving 16.4g total fat (6.8g saturated fat); 2094kJ (501 cal); 16.4g carbohydrate; 69g protein; 4.6g fibre
suitable to freeze Pack into freezer-proof containers, leaving 2.5cm (1-inch) space to allow for expansion. Seal, label and freeze for up to 3 months. After freezing, scrape the fat from the surface before reheating.

9 brown pickling onions (360g)
1.5kg (3-pound) piece beef sirloin or
  beef blade steak
2 teaspoons cracked black pepper
150g (4½-ounce) piece smoked speck
400g (12½ ounces) baby carrots, trimmed
9 baby new potatoes (360g), halved
3 stalks celery (450g), trimmed,
  chopped coarsely
1 litre (4 cups) chicken stock
6 cloves garlic, peeled
1 sprig fresh rosemary
1 sprig fresh thyme
2 fresh bay leaves
1 tablespoon coarsely chopped fresh
  flat-leaf parsley

French for 'pot on the fire', pot-au-feu is the traditional, classic beef stew loved and enjoyed all over France – this is the French version of 'comfort food'.

prep + cook time 8 hours 30 minutes
serves 8

italian pork and capsicum ragù

2 tablespoons olive oil

1.6kg (3¼-pound) rindless boneless
  pork belly, chopped coarsely

4 italian-style thin pork sausages (310g)

3 medium red capsicums (bell peppers)
  (600g), sliced thickly

2 medium brown onions (300g), sliced thinly

1.2kg (2½ pounds) canned white beans,
  rinsed, drained

6 cloves garlic, crushed

400g (12½ ounces) canned diced tomatoes

1¼ cups (310ml) salt-reduced
  chicken stock

1 tablespoon tomato paste

1 teaspoon dried oregano

½ teaspoon chilli flakes

¼ cup loosely packed fresh oregano leaves

1 Heat oil in large frying pan; cook pork, in batches, until browned. Transfer to 4.5-litre (18-cup) slow cooker.

2 Cook sausages in same pan until browned; transfer to cooker with capsicum, onion, beans, garlic, undrained tomatoes, stock, paste, dried oregano and chilli. Cook, covered, on low, 8 hours.

3 Skim fat from surface. Season ragù to taste; serve sprinkled with fresh oregano.

nutritional count per serving 24.8g total fat (8g saturated fat); 2006kJ (480 cal); 10.9g carbohydrate; 51.6g protein; 5g fibre
tip You can quickly peel the capsicum with a vegetable peeler if you don't like the skin peeling off when it's cooked.
suitable to freeze at the end of step 2. Pack into freezer-proof containers, leaving 2.5cm (1-inch) space to allow for expansion. Seal, label and freeze for up to 3 months. Sprinkle with oregano after reheating.

In Italy, ragù is a meat-based sauce that traditionally is served with pasta.

prep + cook time 6 hours 30 minutes
serves 12

french onion lamb chops

1 Trim excess fat from lamb. Toss lamb in flour to coat, shake off excess. Heat oil in large frying pan; cook lamb, in batches, until browned.

2 Place 4 lamb chops into 4.5-litre (18-cup) slow cooker. Sprinkle one-third of the soup mix then one-third of the leek and celery over the chops. Repeat layering with remaining lamb, soup mix, leek and celery. Pour stock into cooker. Cook, covered, on low, 6 hours.

3 Remove lamb from cooker; cover to keep warm. Skim fat from surface of sauce; season to taste. Serve lamb and sauce sprinkled with parsley.

nutritional count per serving 8.5g total fat (2.9g saturated fat); 765kJ (183 cal); 5.8g carbohydrate; 19.9g protein; 2.2g fibre
tip Lamb shoulder chops and chump chops are also suitable for this recipe.
serving suggestion Serve with mashed or roast potatoes, and steamed green beans.
suitable to freeze Pack chops into freezer-proof containers; pour sauce over the chops, leaving 2.5cm (1 inch) space to allow for expansion. Seal, label and freeze for up to 3 months. Sprinkle over parsley after reheating.

12 lamb forequarter chops (2kg)
2 tablespoons plain (all-purpose) flour
2 tablespoons olive oil
80g (2½ ounces) packaged french onion soup mix
2 medium leeks (700g), sliced thinly
3 stalks celery (450g), trimmed, chopped coarsely
2 cups (500ml) salt-reduced chicken stock
¼ cup coarsely chopped fresh flat-leaf parsley

Accompaniments
COUSCOUS, GRAINS & PULSES

prep + cook time 20 minutes serves 6

SOFT POLENTA

Boil 3 cups water and 2 cups
vegetable stock in large saucepan.
Gradually add 2 cups polenta,
stirring constantly. Reduce heat;
simmer, stirring, about 10 minutes
or until polenta thickens. Add
1 cup milk and ¼ cup finely
grated parmesan cheese; stir
until cheese melts. Season to taste.

nutritional count per serving
4.2g total fat (2.1g saturated fat);
1016kJ (243 cal); 41.7g carbohydrate;
8.2g protein; 1.6g fibre

prep time 15 minutes serves 4

PRESERVED LEMON AND MINT COUSCOUS

Combine 1 cup couscous with 1 cup
boiling water in medium heatproof
bowl, cover; stand about 5 minutes or
until water is absorbed, fluffing with
fork occasionally. Stir in 1 teaspoon
ground cumin, 2 tablespoons finely
chopped preserved lemon rind, ½ cup
raisins, 1 cup coarsely chopped fresh
mint and ¼ cup lemon juice. Season
to taste.

nutritional count per serving 0.7g total fat
(0.1g saturated fat); 1066kJ (255 cal);
52.8g carbohydrate; 7.4g protein; 2.5g fibre

prep + cook time 15 minutes serves 6

OLIVE AND PARSLEY COUSCOUS

Bring 1½ cups vegetable stock to the
boil in medium saucepan. Remove
from heat; stir in 1½ cups couscous
and 30g (1 ounce) butter. Cover;
stand about 5 minutes or until liquid
is absorbed, fluffing with fork
occasionally. Stir in 1 cup seeded
kalamata olives and ½ cup chopped
fresh flat-leaf parsley. Season to taste.

nutritional count per serving 4.9g total fat
(2.9g saturated fat); 1074kJ (257 cal);
45.5g carbohydrate; 6.8g protein; 1g fibre

prep + cook time 20 minutes serves 4

SPICED LENTILS

Cook 1½ cups red lentils in large saucepan of boiling water until tender; drain. Melt 25g (¾ ounce) butter in large frying pan; cook 1 finely chopped small brown onion, 1 crushed garlic clove, ½ teaspoon each ground cumin and coriander, ¼ teaspoon each ground turmeric and cayenne pepper, stirring, until onion softens. Add lentils, ½ cup chicken stock and 25g (¾ ounce) butter; cook, stirring, until hot. Remove from heat, stir in 2 tablespoons coarsely chopped fresh flat-leaf parsley. Season to taste.

nutritional count per serving 11.9g total fat (7g saturated fat); 1354kJ (324 cal); 29.9g carbohydrate; 18.9g protein; 10.8g fibre

prep + cook time 1 hour 30 minutes serves 4

MIXED DHAL

Heat 40g (1½ ounces) ghee in large pan; cook 1 finely chopped brown onion and 2 crushed garlic cloves until onion softens. Add 2 teaspoons ground turmeric, 1½ tablespoons black mustard seeds and 1 tablespoon each ground cumin and coriander; cook until fragrant. Stir in ½ cup brown lentils, ⅓ cup each red lentils, yellow split peas and green split peas, 2 cups vegetable stock, 1½ cups water and undrained 400g (12½ ounces) canned crushed tomatoes; simmer, covered, stirring occasionally, about 1 hour or until lentils are tender. Add ⅔ cup coconut cream; stir over low heat until hot. Season to taste.

nutritional count per serving 18.4g total fat (12.5g saturated fat); 1898kJ (454 cal); 42.6g carbohydrate; 23.3g protein; 11.2g fibre

prep time 30 minutes (+ refrigeration) serves 4

TABBOULEH

Place ¼ cup burghul in shallow medium bowl. Halve 3 medium tomatoes; scoop pulp from tomato over burghul. Chop tomato flesh finely; spread over burghul. Cover; refrigerate 1 hour. Combine burghul mixture in large bowl with 3 cups coarsely chopped fresh flat-leaf parsley, 3 finely chopped green onions (scallions), ½ cup coarsely chopped fresh mint, 1 crushed garlic clove, ¼ cup lemon juice and ¼ cup olive oil. Season to taste.

nutritional count per serving 14.2g total fat (2g saturated fat); 790kJ (189 cal); 9.4g carbohydrate; 3.6g protein; 5.9g fibre

slow cooker
Desserts

We were pleasantly surprised at the range of desserts that can be successfully cooked in a slow cooker – steamed puddings are winners – just check that the dishes are a snug fit. The crème caramel, and a variation of bread and butter custard, also worked a treat.

rich chocolate cake (recipe page 110)

Grease a pudding steamer or heatproof china bowl; line the base with a round of baking paper, cut to fit.

Combine the chocolate and butter in a large saucepan; stir constantly over a low heat until smooth.

Remove the chocolate mixture from the heat, stir in egg yolks and brandy, then ground almonds and sifted flour.

prep + cook time 2 hours 30 minutes (+ cooling) **serves** 12

rich chocolate cake

nutritional count per serving
22.7g total fat (14.8g saturated fat);
1400kJ (335 cal); 26.7g carbohydrate;
5.6g protein; 2.5g fibre
serving suggestion Serve with whipped cream and/or ice-cream.
un-iced cake suitable to freeze

(photograph page 109)

180g (5½ ounces) dark eating (semi-sweet) chocolate, chopped coarsely
60g (2 ounces) butter, chopped coarsely
5 eggs, separated
1 tablespoon brandy
½ cup (60g) ground almonds
¼ cup (35g) plain (all-purpose) flour
⅓ cup (75g) caster (superfine) sugar
125g (4 ounces) fresh raspberries

chocolate ganache
½ cup (125ml) pouring cream
180g (5½ ounces) dark eating (semi-sweet) chocolate, chopped finely

Beat the egg whites in a medium bowl with an electric mixer until soft peaks form; add sugar, beat until dissolved.

Fold half the egg white mixture into the cooled chocolate mixture, then fold in remaining egg white mixture.

Spoon the chocolate mixture into the prepared steamer; do not cover the steamer with foil or a lid.

There's no need to cover the pudding steamer with foil or a lid because it is covered when the lid is placed on the cooker.

1 Grease 2-litre (8-cup) pudding steamer; line base with baking paper.
2 Stir chocolate and butter in large saucepan over low heat until smooth. Remove from heat; cool 10 minutes. Stir in egg yolks and brandy, then ground almonds and sifted flour.
3 Beat egg whites in medium bowl with electric mixer until soft peaks form. Add sugar; beat until sugar dissolves. Fold egg white mixture into chocolate mixture, in two batches. Spoon mixture into steamer.
4 Place steamer, without lid, in 4.5-litre (18-cup) slow cooker; pour enough boiling water into cooker to come halfway up side of steamer. Cook, covered, on high, about 2 hours or until cake feels firm.
5 Remove steamer from cooker. Turn cake immediately onto baking-paper-lined wire rack to cool.
6 Meanwhile, make chocolate ganache.
7 Spread cake with chocolate ganache; top with berries.

CHOCOLATE GANACHE
Bring cream to the boil in small saucepan. Remove from heat; add chocolate, stir until smooth. Stand at room temperature until spreadable.

prep + cook time 2 hours 20 minutes (+ refrigeration) makes 6

passionfruit crème caramels

nutritional count per crème caramel
19.1g total fat (11.1g saturated fat);
1371kJ (328 cal); 34.2g carbohydrate;
6.6g protein; 0.9g fibre
not suitable to freeze

½ cup (110g) caster (superfine) sugar
¼ cup (60ml) water
2 tablespoons passionfruit pulp
1 cup (250ml) milk
¾ cup (180ml) pouring cream
2 x 5cm (2-inch) pieces lemon rind
3 eggs
2 egg yolks
⅓ cup (75g) caster (superfine) sugar, extra

1 Stir sugar and the water in small saucepan over high heat, without boiling, until sugar dissolves; bring to the boil. Boil, uncovered, without stirring, until mixture is deep caramel in colour. Remove from heat; allow bubbles to subside, gently stir in passionfruit pulp. Divide toffee mixture into six greased ½-cup (125ml) metal moulds. Place moulds in 4.5-litre (18-cup) slow cooker.
2 Meanwhile, combine milk, cream and rind in medium saucepan; bring to the boil. Whisk eggs, egg yolks and extra sugar in large bowl until combined; gradually whisk in hot milk mixture. Strain mixture into large jug; discard rind. Pour mixture into moulds. Pour enough boiling water into cooker to come halfway up sides of moulds.
3 Cook, covered, on low, about 1½ hours or until crème caramels feel firm. Remove moulds from cooker. Cover moulds; refrigerate overnight.
4 Gently ease crème caramels from sides of moulds; invert onto serving plates.

prep + cook time 2 hours 15 minutes (+ cooling & refrigeration) serves 8

sour cream cheesecake

nutritional count per serving
38.7g total fat (24.2g saturated fat);
2119kJ (507 cal); 33.2g carbohydrate;
8.6g protein; 0.4g fibre
serving suggestion Serve with double
cream, some sliced strawberries and
drizzled with passionfruit pulp.
not suitable to freeze

500g (1 pound) cream cheese, softened
⅔ cup (150g) caster (superfine) sugar
1 teaspoon vanilla extract
2 eggs
½ cup (120g) sour cream
¼ cup (60ml) lemon juice
1 tablespoon plain (all-purpose) flour
125g (4 ounces) granita biscuits
80g (2½ ounces) butter, melted

The baking paper strips are used to help remove the cheesecake from the steamer once it's been refrigerated overnight. Place the steamer upside down on a serving plate, gently pull on the paper strips and the cheesecake will ease away from the sides of the steamer.

1 Grease 2-litre (8-cup) pudding steamer. Cut two long strips of baking paper; place strips on inside of steamer, crossing over at the bottom, extending 5cm (2 inches) over side of steamer (see note).
2 Beat cream cheese, sugar and vanilla in small bowl with electric mixer until smooth. Add eggs, sour cream, juice and flour; beat until smooth. Spoon mixture into steamer.
3 Place steamer, without lid, in 4.5-litre (18-cup) slow cooker; pour enough boiling water into cooker to come halfway up side of steamer. Cook, covered, on low, 1 hour.
4 Meanwhile, blend or process biscuits until fine. Add butter; process until combined. Remove lid from cooker. Press biscuit mixture on top of cheesecake; top with three layers of absorbent paper. Cook, covered, on low, for a further 45 minutes.
5 Remove steamer from cooker; cool. Cover; refrigerate overnight.

Champagne and rosewater poached pears (recipe page 118)

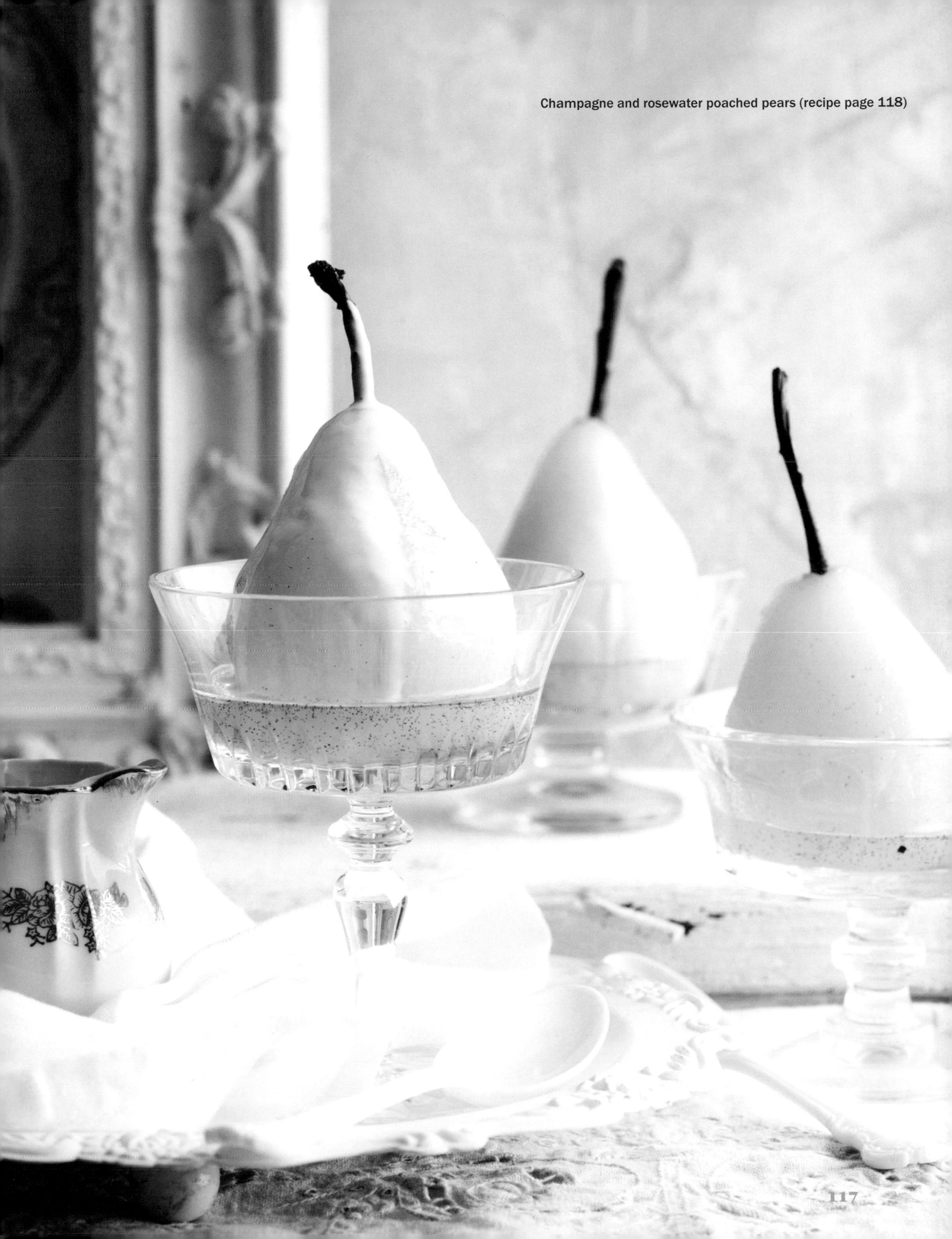

prep + cook time 4 hours 55 minutes (+ cooling) serves 6

Champagne and rosewater poached pears

6 medium firm pears (1.4kg)

3 cups (750ml) Champagne

1 cup (220g) caster (superfine) sugar

4 x 5cm (2-inch) strips lemon rind

3 teaspoons rosewater

1 vanilla bean

(photograph page 117)

1 Peel pears, leaving stems intact.

2 Combine Champagne, sugar, rind and rosewater in 4.5-litre (18-cup) slow cooker. Halve vanilla bean lengthways, scrape seeds into cooker; add bean.

3 Lay pears down in cooker to submerge in champagne mixture. Cook, covered, on high, about 4½ hours or until pears are tender.

4 Place 1 cup of the poaching liquid in small saucepan; bring to the boil. Boil, uncovered, about 7 minutes or until syrup is reduced by about half; cool.

5 Place pears in large deep bowl; add remaining poaching liquid, cool.

6 Serve pears drizzled with syrup.

nutritional count per serving 0.2g total fat (0g saturated fat); 1342kJ (321 cal); 61.5g carbohydrate; 0.8g protein; 3.2g fibre

tips Store any leftover poaching liquid in the refrigerator for up to 1 month. Use for poaching more pears or stone fruit. We used packham pears in this recipe.

serving suggestion Serve with cream, ice-cream or custard.

not suitable to freeze

prep + cook time 2 hours 50 minutes serves 6

nutty banana self-saucing pudding

90g (3 ounces) butter, chopped coarsely

¾ cup (180ml) milk

1 teaspoon vanilla extract

½ cup (110g) firmly packed
  light brown sugar

1⅔ cups (250g) self-raising flour

½ cup mashed overripe banana

⅓ cup (40g) coarsely chopped
  roasted pecans

1 egg, beaten lightly

1 cup (220g) firmly packed light brown
  sugar, extra

2½ cups (625ml) boiling water

2 tablespoons golden syrup or treacle

1 Grease 4.5-litre (18-cup) slow cooker bowl.

2 Heat butter and milk in medium saucepan until butter is melted. Remove from heat; cool 5 minutes. Stir in extract and sugar, then sifted flour, banana, nuts and egg. Spread mixture into cooker bowl.

3 Sprinkle extra sugar evenly over mixture. Gently pour the combined boiling water and golden syrup evenly over mixture. Cook, covered, on high, about 2½ hours or until pudding feels firm.

4 Remove bowl from cooker. Stand pudding 10 minutes before serving.

nutritional count per serving 19.7g total fat (9.5g saturated fat); 2420kJ (579 cal); 95.1g carbohydrate; 7.4g protein; 2.6g fibre

serving suggestion Serve hot or warm, with cream, ice-cream or custard.

not suitable to freeze

nutty banana self-saucing pudding

prep + cook time 4 hours (+ standing) **serves** 6

rhubarb and orange compote

nutritional count per serving
20.5g total fat (8.8g saturated fat);
1580kJ (378 cal); 37.7g carbohydrate;
7.7g protein; 6.3g fibre
not suitable to freeze

16 large trimmed stems rhubarb (1kg),
  chopped coarsely
1 teaspoon finely grated orange rind
2 large oranges (600g), peeled, sliced
  thickly
⅔ cup (150g) raw caster (superfine) sugar
¼ cup (60ml) cranberry juice
1 teaspoon each ground ginger and
  cinnamon
1 cup (80g) flaked almonds, roasted

cinnamon yogurt cream
½ cup (125ml) thick (double) cream
½ cup (140g) greek-style yogurt
½ teaspoon cinnamon sugar

1 Grease 4.5-litre (18-cup) slow cooker bowl.
2 Combine rhubarb, rind, orange, sugar, juice and spices in cooker. Cook, covered, on low, about 3½ hours or until rhubarb is tender. Remove bowl from cooker. Stand 20 minutes before serving.
3 Meanwhile, make cinnamon yogurt cream.
4 Divide rhubarb mixture into serving bowls; top with cinnamon yogurt cream and nuts.

CINNAMON YOGURT CREAM
Combine ingredients in small bowl.

prep + cook time 1 hour 30 minutes
makes 4

delicious lemony lime puddings

90g (3 ounces) butter, melted
1 teaspoon finely grated lemon rind
½ teaspoon finely grated lime rind
¾ cup (165g) caster (superfine) sugar
2 eggs, separated
⅓ cup (50g) self-raising flour
2 tablespoons lemon juice
1 tablespoon lime juice
1 cup (250ml) milk

1 Grease four ¾-cup (180ml) deep heatproof dishes (ensure the dishes will fit into your slow cooker bowl).
2 Combine butter, rinds, sugar and egg yolks in medium bowl. Whisk in sifted flour, then juices. Gradually whisk in milk; mixture should be smooth and runny.
3 Beat egg whites in small bowl with electric mixer until soft peaks form; fold into lemon mixture, in two batches. Divide mixture between dishes.
4 Place dishes in 4.5-litre (18-cup) slow cooker; pour enough boiling water into cooker to come halfway up sides of dishes. Cook, covered, on high, about 1 hour or until firm. Remove dishes from cooker. Stand puddings 10 minutes before serving.

nutritional count per pudding 23.7g total fat (14.6g saturated fat); 1873kJ (448 cal); 53.8g carbohydrate; 6.9g protein; 0.5g fibre
serving suggestion Serve with warm, dusted with a little sifted icing sugar (confectioners' sugar) and accompany with double (thick) cream.
not suitable to freeze

prep + cook time 3 hours serves 6

mixed berry pudding

1 Grease 4.5-litre (18-cup) slow cooker bowl.
2 Heat butter and milk in medium saucepan over low heat until butter is melted. Remove from heat; cool 5 minutes. Stir in extract and sugar, then sifted flour and egg.
3 Sprinkle berries over base of cooker bowl; drop tablespoons of jam over berries. Spread pudding mixture over berry mixture. Gently pour the boiling water evenly over pudding mixture. Cook, covered, on high, about 2½ hours or until centre of pudding feels firm.
4 Remove bowl from cooker. Stand pudding 10 minutes before serving.

nutritional count per serving 15.2g total fat (9.2g saturated fat); 1935kJ (463 cal); 71.8g carbohydrate; 7.4g protein; 6.4g fibre
serving suggestion Serve warm, dusted with a little sifted icing sugar (confectioners' sugar) and accompany with custard.
not suitable to freeze

90g (3 ounces) butter
¾ cup (180ml) milk
1 teaspoon vanilla extract
½ cup (110g) caster (superfine) sugar
1⅔ cups (250g) self-raising flour
1 egg, beaten lightly
500g (1 pound) frozen mixed berries
½ cup (160g) raspberry jam
2 cups (500ml) boiling water

prep + cook time 3 hours 15 minutes (+ standing) **serves** 8

croissant custard pudding with strawberries

nutritional count per serving
44.7g total fat (28.8g saturated fat);
2658kJ (636 cal); 51.4g carbohydrate;
7.9g protein; 1.7g fibre
serving suggestion Serve pudding with
ice-cream and/or cream.
not suitable to freeze

4 croissants (200g)
½ cup (160g) strawberry jam
80g (2½ ounces) white eating chocolate,
  chopped finely
2½ cups (625ml) milk
2⅓ cups (600ml) pouring cream
½ cup (110g) caster (superfine) sugar
1 teaspoon vanilla extract
6 eggs

macerated strawberries
250g (8 ounces) strawberries, halved
1 tablespoon orange-flavoured liqueur
1 tablespoon icing (confectioners') sugar

It's important not to lift the lid during the cooking of the pudding, as the condensation runs down the side of the cooker and causes damp patches on the pudding.

1 Grease 4.5-litre (18-cup) slow cooker bowl.
2 Split croissants in half; spread cut-sides with jam; sprinkle chocolate over half the croissants, sandwich with remaining croissants. Place croissants in cooker.
3 Combine milk, cream, sugar and extract in medium saucepan; bring to the boil. Whisk eggs in large bowl; gradually whisk in hot milk mixture. Pour custard over croissants; stand 10 minutes.
4 Cook, covered, on low, about 2 hours 45 minutes, or until firm (do not lift the lid during the cooking process, see note).
5 Meanwhile, make macerated strawberries.
6 Remove bowl from cooker. Stand pudding 5 minutes before serving. Serve pudding with macerated strawberries and drizzled with a little extra cream.

MACERATED STRAWBERRIES
Combine ingredients in medium bowl; stand 30 minutes.

prep + cook time 5 hours 30 minutes **serves** 12

sticky date and fig steamed pudding

nutritional count per serving
24.9g total fat (15.9g saturated fat);
2174kJ (520 cal); 70.6g carbohydrate;
4.4g protein; 4.3g fibre
pudding suitable to freeze

2 cups (300g) finely chopped seeded
  dried dates
½ cup (100g) finely chopped dried figs
1 cup (250ml) water
1 cup (220g) firmly packed
  light brown sugar
90g (3 ounces) butter, chopped coarsely
1 teaspoon bicarbonate of soda
  (baking soda)
2 eggs, beaten lightly
¾ cup (110g) plain (all-purpose) flour
¾ cup (110g) self-raising flour

butterscotch sauce
¾ cup (165g) firmly packed
  light brown sugar
1 cup (250ml) pouring cream
125g (4 ounces) unsalted butter,
  chopped coarsely

1 Combine fruit, the water, sugar and butter in medium saucepan; stir over heat until butter melts and sugar dissolves. Bring to the boil. Reduce heat; simmer, uncovered, 5 minutes. Transfer mixture to large heatproof bowl, stir in soda; cool 10 minutes.
2 Stir eggs and sifted dry ingredients into fruit mixture.
3 Grease 2-litre (8-cup) pudding steamer; spoon mixture into steamer. Top with pleated baking paper and foil; secure with kitchen string or lid.
4 Place steamer in 4.5-litre (18-cup) slow cooker; pour enough boiling water into cooker to come halfway up side of steamer. Cook, covered, on high, 5 hours, replenishing with boiling water as necessary to maintain level.
5 Remove pudding from cooker. Stand 10 minutes before turning onto plate.
6 Meanwhile, make butterscotch sauce.
7 Serve pudding with butterscotch sauce, and a dollop of thick cream, if you like.

BUTTERSCOTCH SAUCE
Stir ingredients in medium saucepan over heat, without boiling, until sugar dissolves; bring to the boil. Reduce heat; simmer, uncovered, 2 minutes.

Accompaniments
CREAMS, CUSTARDS & SAUCES

prep time 10 minutes **makes** 1 cup

STRAWBERRY COULIS

Push 300g (9½ ounces) thawed frozen strawberries through fine sieve into small bowl; discard seeds. Stir in 1 tablespoon sifted icing (confectioners') sugar.

nutritional count per tablespoon
0.3g total fat (0 saturated fat); 42kJ (10 cal); 1.6g carbohydrate; 0.4g protein; 0.6g fibre

prep + cook time 30 minutes (+ refrigeration)
makes 1½ cups

CRÈME ANGLAISE

Split 1 vanilla bean in half lengthways; scrape seeds into medium saucepan, add pod, 1½ cups milk and 1 tablespoon caster (superfine) sugar. Boil, then strain into large jug. Discard pod. Whisk 4 egg yolks and ¼ cup caster (superfine) sugar in medium heatproof bowl set over medium saucepan of simmering water until thick and creamy; gradually whisk in hot milk mixture. Return custard mixture to pan; stir, over low heat, until mixture is thick enough to coat the back of a spoon. Refrigerate custard about 1 hour or until cold.

nutritional count per tablespoon 2.1g total fat (0.9g saturated fat); 184kJ (44 cal); 5.2g carbohydrate; 1.4g protein; 0 fibre

prep + cook time 15 minutes **makes** 1 cup

CHOCOLATE FUDGE SAUCE

Stir 20g (¾ ounce) butter and 200g (6½ ounces) coarsely chopped dark eating (semi-sweet) chocolate in small heatproof bowl set over small saucepan of simmering water until smooth. Add ¼ teaspoon vanilla extract and ½ cup pouring cream; stir until combined. Serve sauce warm.

nutritional count per tablespoon
10.6g total fat (6.7g saturated fat); 585kJ (140 cal); 10.7g carbohydrate; 1.1g protein; 0.2g fibre

prep time 20 minutes makes 1 cup

HAZELNUT CREAM

Beat 1 tablespoon hazelnut-flavoured liqueur, ⅔ cup pouring cream and 1 tablespoon caster (superfine) sugar in small bowl with electric mixer until soft peaks form; stir in ⅓ cup coarsely chopped roasted hazelnuts.

nutritional count per tablespoon
8.1g total fat (3.9g saturated fat); 380kJ (91 cal); 2.8g carbohydrate; 0.8g protein; 0.4g fibre

prep + cook time 20 minutes (+ refrigeration)
makes 2 cups

COFFEE LIQUEUR SAUCE

Combine ¼ cup pouring cream and ⅔ cup freshly brewed strong coffee in small saucepan; stir over heat, without boiling, until hot. Remove from heat; add 250g (8 ounces) coarsely chopped white eating chocolate, whisk until smooth. Stir in 1 tablespoon coffee-flavoured liqueur. Transfer sauce to small bowl; cover, refrigerate about 30 minutes, stirring occasionally.

nutritional count per tablespoon 4.5g total fat (2.9g saturated fat); 297kJ (71 cal); 6.2g carbohydrate; 0.8g protein; 0 fibre

prep + cook time 10 minutes makes 3½ cups

BRANDY CUSTARD

Combine 1¼ cups (310ml) thickened (heavy) cream, 1 tablespoon sifted icing (confectioners') sugar and seeds from 1 vanilla bean in small bowl; beat with electric mixer until soft peaks form. Stir 500g (1 pound) thick custard and 2 tablespoons brandy in small saucepan over low heat until warm. Transfer to large bowl; gently fold cream mixture into warm custard.

nutritional count per tablespoon 3.1g total fat (2g saturated fat); 167kJ (40 cal); 2.2g carbohydrate; 0.5g protein; 0g fibre

tips It is fine to use just 1 x 300ml carton of cream for this recipe.

129

ON THE STOVE TOP

chicken, chorizo and okra gumbo
(recipe page 134)

133

Make the broth, strain it though a muslin-lined colander into a large heatproof bowl; discard the solids.

When the chicken is cool enough to handle, discard all the skin and bones; using fingers, shred the meat coarsely.

Melt the butter in a large saucepan; cook the extra onion and garlic, stirring, until the onion softens.

prep + cook time 3 hours 15 minutes **serves** 8

chicken, chorizo and okra gumbo

nutritional count per serving
26.8g total fat (5.7g saturated fat); 2011kJ (481 cal); 30.5g carbohydrate; 27.8g protein; 3.9g fibre
tips If you want to cook this gumbo a day ahead, the flavours will meld and deepen, making the soup even more delicious. Follow the recipe through to the end of step 2, then cool the soup, cover and refrigerate it overnight.
not suitable to freeze

(photograph page 133)

3 litres (12 cups) water
1.5kg (3-pound) chicken
2 medium carrots (240g), chopped coarsely
2 stalks celery (300g), trimmed, chopped coarsely
1 medium brown onion (150g), chopped coarsely
12 black peppercorns
1 dried bay leaf
60g (2 ounces) butter
1 small brown onion (80g), chopped finely, extra
2 cloves garlic, crushed

1 medium red capsicum (bell pepper) (200g), chopped finely
2 teaspoons dried oregano
1 teaspoon sweet paprika
¼ teaspoon cayenne pepper
¼ teaspoon ground clove
¼ cup (35g) plain (all-purpose) flour
¼ cup (70g) tomato paste
400g (12½ ounces) canned crushed tomatoes
100g (3 ounces) fresh okra, halved diagonally
1 cup (200g) white medium-grain rice
1 cured chorizo sausage (170g), sliced thinly

Add capsicum, herbs and spices, stir constantly over heat until the mixture becomes fragrant.

Stir the flour and paste into the pan; cook, stirring over heat about 1 minute, or until mixture thickens slightly.

Stir in the okra and rice; simmer, uncovered, stirring occasionally, about 15 minutes, or until the rice is tender.

Gumbo, an African word for okra, is basically any Cajun (southern US) soup that is thickened with a roux (a flour/butter mix); its specific content is left up to the individual, but usually includes sausage and rice. Okra, a distinctively textured green vegetable, is often used in stews and casseroles.

1   Place the water in large saucepan with chicken, carrot, celery, onion, peppercorns and bay leaf; bring to the boil. Reduce heat; simmer, covered, 1½ hours.
2   Remove chicken from pan. Strain broth through muslin-lined sieve or colander into large heatproof bowl; discard solids. When chicken is cool enough to handle, remove and discard skin and bones; shred meat coarsely.
3   Melt butter in large saucepan; cook extra onion and garlic, stirring, until onion softens. Add capsicum, herbs and spices; cook, stirring, until fragrant. Add flour and paste; cook, stirring, 1 minute. Gradually stir in reserved broth and undrained tomatoes; bring to the boil, stirring. Stir in okra and rice; simmer, uncovered, stirring occasionally, about 15 minutes or until rice is tender.
4   Heat large oiled frying pan; cook sausage until browned, drain. Add sausage with chicken to gumbo; stir over medium heat until hot. Season to taste.

prep + cook time 2 hours 40 minutes (+ standing) serves 8

harira

nutritional count per serving
8.6g total fat (4g saturated fat);
1095kJ (262 cal); 23.6g carbohydrate;
20.1g protein; 4.8g fibre
suitable to freeze at the end of step 4.
Stir in coriander and juice after reheating.

1 cup (200g) dried chickpeas
  (garbanzo beans)
20g (¾ ounce) butter
2 medium brown onions (300g),
  chopped finely
2 stalks celery (300g), trimmed,
  chopped finely
2 cloves garlic, crushed
4cm (1¾-inch) piece fresh ginger (20g),
  grated
1 teaspoon ground cinnamon
½ teaspoon ground black pepper

pinch saffron threads
500g (1 pound) diced lamb
3 large tomatoes (660g), seeded,
  chopped coarsely
2 litres (8 cups) hot water
½ cup (100g) brown lentils
2 tablespoons plain (all-purpose) flour
½ cup (100g) cooked white long-grain rice
½ cup firmly packed fresh coriander
  (cilantro) leaves
2 tablespoons lemon juice

After sundown during Ramadan, many of the Muslims in Morocco break the day's fast by starting their meal with this hearty, nourishing soup. Recipes vary from family to family, but chickpeas and lamb always feature.

1 Place chickpeas in medium bowl, cover with water, stand overnight; drain. Rinse under cold water; drain.
2 Melt butter in large saucepan; cook onion, celery and garlic, stirring, until onion softens. Add ginger, cinnamon, pepper and saffron; cook, stirring, until fragrant. Add lamb; cook, stirring, about 5 minutes or until lamb is browned. Add chickpeas and tomato; cook, stirring, about 5 minutes or until tomato softens.
3 Stir the water into soup mixture; bring to the boil. Reduce heat; simmer, covered, 45 minutes. Add lentils; simmer, covered, 1 hour.
4 Blend flour with ½ cup of the slightly cooled broth in small bowl; return to pan with rice. Cook, stirring, until soup boils and thickens slightly.
5 Remove from heat; stir in coriander and juice. Season to taste.

prep + cook time 3 hours 30 minutes serves 6

chilli con carne with corn dumplings

nutritional count per serving
28.2g total fat (11.7g saturated fat);
2784kJ (666 cal); 37 carbohydrate;
62.1g protein; 7.4g fibre
not suitable to freeze

2 tablespoons olive oil
1.5kg (3 pounds) chuck steak,
  chopped coarsely
2 medium brown onions (300g),
  chopped coarsely
2 cloves garlic, crushed
1 large green capsicum (bell pepper)
  (350g), chopped coarsely
2 teaspoons each sweet paprika, ground
  cumin and chilli powder
800g (1½ pounds) canned whole peeled
  tomatoes
2 tablespoons tomato paste
1 cup (250ml) beef stock
400g (12½ ounces) canned kidney beans,
  rinsed, drained

corn dumplings
½ cup (75g) self-raising flour
½ cup (85g) polenta
50g (1½ ounces) butter, chopped
1 egg, beaten lightly
¼ cup (30g) coarsely grated cheddar
  cheese
¼ cup coarsely chopped fresh coriander
  (cilantro)
130g (4 ounces) canned corn kernels,
  rinsed, drained
1 tablespoon milk, approximately

1 Heat half the oil in large saucepan; cook steak, in batches, until browned. Remove from pan.
2 Heat remaining oil in same pan; cook onion, garlic and capsicum, stirring, until vegetables soften. Add spices; cook, stirring until fragrant.
3 Return steak to pan with undrained tomatoes, paste and stock; bring to the boil. Reduce heat; simmer, covered, about 2½ hours or until tender.
4 Shred a quarter of the steak coarsely with two forks, add meat to pan with beans; bring to the boil. Simmer, uncovered, 15 minutes. Season to taste.
5 Meanwhile, make corn dumplings. Drop level tablespoons of dumpling mixture, about 2cm (¾ inch) apart, on top of steak mixture. Simmer, covered, about 20 minutes or until dumplings are cooked through.

CORN DUMPLINGS
Place flour and polenta in medium bowl; rub in butter. Stir in egg, cheese, coriander, corn and enough milk to mix to a soft, sticky dough.

prep + cook time 2 hours 40 minutes
serves 8

pork with beans and beer

3 cloves garlic, crushed

½ teaspoon freshly ground black pepper

1.8kg (3½ pounds) pork neck

1 tablespoon olive oil

3 rindless bacon slices (195g),
   chopped finely

2 medium brown onions (300g),
   sliced thinly

2 teaspoons caraway seeds

1½ cups (375ml) beer

1 cup (200g) dried haricot beans

1½ cups (375ml) chicken stock

¼ small (300g) white cabbage,
   shredded finely

1 Rub combined garlic and pepper all over pork. Secure pork with kitchen
   string at 2cm (¾-inch) intervals to make an even shape.
2 Heat oil in large flameproof casserole dish; cook pork until browned all
   over. Remove from dish.
3 Cook bacon, onion and seeds in same dish, stirring, until onion is soft and
   bacon is browned lightly.
4 Return pork to dish with beer, beans and stock; simmer, covered, about
   2 hours or until beans and pork are tender. Remove pork from dish. Add
   cabbage; cook, stirring, until just wilted.

nutritional count per serving 24.4g total fat (7.8g saturated fat); 2261kJ (541 cal);
13.9g carbohydrate; 59.8g protein; 6.7g fibre
not suitable to freeze

prep + cook time 2 hour 30 minutes
serves 4

minted broad bean and ham soup

1 Heat oil in large saucepan; cook onion, celery, carrot and garlic, stirring, until vegetables soften. Add ham hock and the water; bring to the boil. Reduce heat; simmer, covered, 1½ hours. Uncover; simmer 30 minutes.
2 Meanwhile, place beans in medium heatproof bowl, cover with boiling water; stand 5 minutes, drain. Peel away grey skins.
3 Remove ham hock from soup; when cool enough to handle, remove meat from bone, shred coarsely. Discard skin and bone.
4 Add beans to soup; simmer, uncovered, 5 minutes or until beans are tender. Cool soup 10 minutes.
5 Using hand-held blender, blend soup, in pan, until soup is almost smooth. Return ham meat to soup with juice; cook, stirring, until hot. Season to taste.
6 Serve soup sprinkled with mint.

nutritional count per serving 7.4g total fat (2g saturated fat); 890kJ (213 cal); 13.4g carbohydrate; 17.7g protein; 11.4g fibre
suitable to freeze at the end of step 5. Sprinkle with mint after reheating.

2 teaspoons olive oil
1 large brown onion (200g), chopped coarsely
2 stalks celery (300g), chopped coarsely
1 medium carrot (120g), chopped coarsely
2 cloves garlic, crushed
1kg (2-pound) ham hock
2 litres (8 cups) water
3 cups (450g) frozen broad beans
1 tablespoon lemon juice
⅓ cup finely chopped fresh mint

prep + cook time 2 hours 40 minutes **serves** 6

thai-style beef curry

nutritional count per serving
38.7g total fat (28g saturated fat);
2809kJ (672 cal); 33.8g carbohydrate;
43.7g protein; 7.8g fibre
not suitable to freeze

1 tablespoon peanut oil
3 large brown onions (600g), sliced thickly
2 cloves garlic, crushed
4cm (1¾-inch) piece fresh ginger (20g), grated
2 fresh long red chillies, chopped finely
1 tablespoon finely chopped coriander root and stem mixture
1kg (2 pound) gravy beef, chopped coarsely
2 cups (500ml) beef stock
10cm (4-inch) stick fresh lemon grass (20g), halved lengthways, bruised
1 tablespoon tamarind concentrate

1 tablespoon grated palm sugar
3¼ cups (810ml) coconut milk
1 tablespoon fish sauce
800g (1½ pounds) baby new potatoes, halved
1 large red capsicum (bell pepper) (350g), chopped coarsely
2 teaspoons lime juice
3 green onions (scallions), sliced thinly
1 cup (80g) bean sprouts
1 fresh long red chilli, sliced thinly
⅓ cup loosely packed fresh coriander (cilantro) leaves

1   Heat oil in large saucepan; cook brown onion, garlic, ginger, chopped chilli and coriander root and stem mixture, stirring, until onion softens.
2   Add beef, 1½ cups stock, lemon grass, tamarind, sugar, half the coconut milk and half the sauce; bring to the boil. Reduce heat; simmer, uncovered, about 1½ hours or until beef is tender.
3   Add potato, capsicum, and the remaining stock and coconut milk; bring to the boil. Reduce heat, simmer, uncovered, about 30 minutes or until potato is tender.
4   Stir in juice, green onion and remaining sauce. Season to taste.
5   Serve curry sprinkled with remaining ingredients.

prep + cook time 1 hour 30 minutes serves 6

vegetable dhansak

nutritional count per serving
3.7g total fat (0.6 saturated fat);
1614kJ (386 cal); 74.4g carbohydrate;
13.4g protein; 8.9g fibre
not suitable to freeze

1 large eggplant (500g), chopped coarsely
500g (1 pound) pumpkin, chopped coarsely
2 medium tomatoes (300g), peeled,
   chopped coarsely
1 large brown onion (200g), sliced thinly
3 cups (750ml) water
400g (12½ ounces) canned chickpeas
   (garbanzo beans), rinsed, drained
400g (12½ ounces) canned brown lentils,
   rinsed, drained
1 tablespoon garam masala
2 cups (400g) basmati rice
2 teaspoons vegetable oil
2 medium brown onions (300g),
   sliced thinly, extra
¼ cup firmly packed fresh coriander
   (cilantro) leaves

masala paste
3 dried small red chillies
2 fresh long green chillies
2cm (¾-inch) piece fresh ginger (10g),
   quartered
3 cloves garlic, quartered
½ cup loosely packed fresh coriander
   (cilantro) leaves
2 tablespoons hot water

Dhansak is an Indian adaptation of a famous festive dish of the Parsi community of the Indian subcontinent; it always consists of several types of pulses and vegetables, and is served with rice. The Parsi often add mutton to the dish.

1 Blend or process ingredients for masala paste until smooth.
2 Place eggplant, pumpkin, tomato, onion and the water in large saucepan; bring to the boil. Reduce heat; simmer, covered, 15 minutes, stirring occasionally. Drain mixture through sieve over large bowl; reserve 1½ cups of the cooking liquid, discard remainder.
3 Combine half the chickpeas, half the lentils and half the vegetable mixture in another large bowl; mash lightly.
4 Dry-fry garam masala and masala paste in same cleaned pan, stirring, until fragrant. Add all the chickpeas, all the lentils, the vegetable mixtures and reserved liquid to pan; bring to the boil. Reduce heat; simmer, uncovered, 20 minutes, stirring occasionally. Season to taste.
5 Meanwhile, cook rice in large saucepan of boiling water until tender; drain.
6 Heat oil in medium saucepan; cook extra onion, stirring, 10 minutes or until browned. Sprinkle onion and coriander over dhansak. Serve with rice, and lemon, if you like.

prep + cook time 2 hours 30 minutes
serves 4

lamb and macadamia curry

1 cup (140g) roasted unsalted macadamias

2 tablespoons vegetable oil

800g (1½ pounds) diced lamb shoulder

1 medium brown onion (150g), chopped
    coarsely

1 clove garlic, crushed

2 fresh small red thai (serrano) chillies,
    chopped finely

2cm (¾-inch) piece fresh ginger (10g),
    grated

1 teaspoon each ground cumin and
    turmeric

½ teaspoon each ground cinnamon,
    cardamom and fennel

400g (12½ ounces) canned diced tomatoes

1⅔ cups (410ml) coconut milk

1 cup (250ml) beef stock

½ cup loosely packed fresh coriander
    (cilantro) leaves

1 Blend half the nuts until finely ground; coarsely chop remaining nuts.

2 Heat half the oil in large saucepan; cook lamb, in batches, until browned.

3 Heat remaining oil in same pan; cook onion, garlic, chilli and ginger, stirring,
   until onion softens. Add spices; cook, stirring, until fragrant. Return lamb to
   pan with ground nuts, undrained tomatoes, coconut milk and stock; bring
   to the boil. Reduce heat; simmer, covered, about 1¼ hours or until lamb is
   tender. Uncover; simmer about 15 minutes or until sauce thickens slightly.
   Season to taste.

4 Serve lamb sprinkled with remaining nuts and coriander.

nutritional count per serving 68.4g total fat (28.4g saturated); 3561kJ (852 cal);
11.6g carbohydrate; 47g protein; 5.9g fibre
suitable to freeze at the end of step 3. Sprinkle with nuts and coriander after reheating.

prep + cook time 2 hours 30 minutes
serves 4

braised beef brisket

1 Heat half the oil in large saucepan; cook beef, in batches, until browned. Remove from pan.
2 Heat remaining oil in same pan; cook onion, garlic and ginger until onion softens.
3 Return beef to pan with sauces, sugar, five-spice, lemon grass and the water; bring to the boil. Reduce heat; simmer, covered, about 1¼ hours or until beef is tender. Discard lemon grass. Add beans and ½ cup of the nuts; simmer, uncovered, 15 minutes. Season to taste.
4 Serve beef, sprinkled with remaining nuts and mint.

nutritional count per serving 35.6g total fat (8.3g saturated); 2458kJ (588 cal); 8.3g carbohydrate; 56.8g protein; 4.2g fibre
suitable to freeze at the end of step 3. Sprinkle beef with nuts and mint after reheating.

2 tablespoons vegetable oil
1kg beef brisket, trimmed, cut into 3cm pieces
1 small brown onion (80g), sliced thinly
2 cloves garlic, crushed
2cm (¾-inch) piece fresh ginger (10g), grated
2 tablespoons fish sauce
1 tablespoon dark soy sauce
1 tablespoon light brown sugar
1 teaspoon five-spice powder
2 x 10cm (4-inch) sticks fresh lemon grass (40g), halved crossways
2 cups (500ml) water
150g (4½ ounces) snake beans, chopped coarsely
¾ cup (105g) crushed peanuts
⅓ cup loosely packed vietnamese mint leaves

prep + cook time 3 hours 20 minutes **serves** 6

osso buco with semi-dried tomatoes and olives

nutritional count per serving
25.2g total fat (8.6g saturated fat);
2771kJ (663 cal); 19.6g carbohydrate;
78.5g protein; 6.2g fibre
suitable to freeze at the end of step 2.

12 pieces veal osso buco (3kg)
¼ cup (35g) plain (all-purpose) flour
¼ cup (60ml) olive oil
40g (1½ ounces) butter
1 medium brown onion (150g),
   chopped coarsely
2 cloves garlic, chopped finely
3 stalks celery (300g), trimmed,
   chopped coarsely
2 large carrots (360g), chopped coarsely
4 medium tomatoes (600g),
   chopped coarsely
2 tablespoons tomato paste
1 cup (250ml) dry white wine

1 cup (250ml) beef stock
400g (12½ ounces) canned crushed
   tomatoes
4 sprigs fresh lemon thyme
½ cup (75g) drained semi-dried tomatoes
¼ cup (60ml) lemon juice
1 tablespoon finely grated lemon rind
½ cup (75g) seeded kalamata olives
gremolata
1 tablespoon finely grated lemon rind
⅓ cup finely chopped fresh flat-leaf parsley
2 cloves garlic, chopped finely

Literally meaning 'bone with a hole', osso buco is filled with rich bone marrow; stand the bones upright to cook so you don't lose the delicious marrow inside.

1 Coat veal in flour; shake off excess. Heat oil in large deep saucepan; cook veal, in batches, until browned. Remove from pan.
2 Melt butter in same pan; cook onion, garlic, celery and carrot, stirring, until vegetables soften. Stir in fresh tomato, tomato paste, wine, stock, undrained tomatoes and thyme. Return veal to pan, fitting pieces upright and tightly together in a single layer; bring to the boil. Reduce heat; simmer, covered, 1¾ hours. Stir in semi-dried tomatoes; simmer, uncovered, about 30 minutes or until veal is tender.
3 Remove veal from pan; cover to keep warm. Bring sauce to the boil; boil, uncovered, about 10 minutes or until sauce thickens slightly. Stir in juice, rind and olives; season to taste.
4 Meanwhile, combine ingredients for gremolata in small bowl. Divide veal between serving plates; top with sauce, sprinkle with gremolata.

prep + cook time 3 hours serves 6

shredded spanish beef

nutritional count per serving
17.5g total fat (4.7g saturated fat);
1969kJ (471 cal); 11 carbohydrate;
64 protein; 6.2g fibre
not suitable to freeze

5 cloves garlic, quartered
1 large carrot (180g), chopped coarsely
1 stalk celery (150g), trimmed,
 chopped coarsely
1.5kg (3 pounds) beef skirt steak
6 black peppercorns
2 teaspoons dried oregano
2 litres (8 cups) water
2 tablespoons olive oil
2 rindless bacon slices (130g),
 chopped finely
3 cloves garlic, extra, crushed
1 small brown onion (80g), chopped finely
½ small green capsicum (bell pepper)
 (75g), chopped finely

1 tablespoon tomato paste
2 tablespoons red wine vinegar
1 medium red capsicum (bell pepper)
 (200g), sliced thickly
1 medium green capsicum (bell pepper)
 (200g), sliced thickly
2 medium brown onions (300g),
 sliced thickly
400g (12½ ounces) canned whole tomatoes
1 teaspoon ground cumin
1 cup (150g) pimiento-stuffed green
 olives, halved
¼ cup (60ml) lemon juice

1 Place quartered garlic, carrot, celery, beef, peppercorns, half the oregano,
   and the water in large deep saucepan; bring to the boil. Reduce heat; simmer,
   uncovered, 2 hours or until beef is tender.
2 Meanwhile, heat half the oil in small frying pan; cook bacon, crushed garlic,
   finely chopped onion and finely chopped capsicum, stirring, until onion softens.
   Stir in paste and vinegar; cook until vinegar evaporates. Cool 10 minutes; blend
   or process until smooth.
3 Remove beef from braising liquid. Strain liquid over large bowl; discard solids.
   Using two forks, shred beef coarsely.
4 Heat remaining oil in same cleaned pan; cook capsicum mixture with thickly
   sliced capsicums and thickly sliced onion, stirring, until vegetables soften.
   Return beef and braising liquid to pan with undrained tomatoes, cumin and
   remaining oregano; bring to the boil. Reduce heat; simmer, uncovered,
   20 minutes. Remove from heat; stir in olives and juice. Season to taste.

Accompaniments
SAUCES, SALSAS & TOPPINGS

prep time 10 minutes serves 4

GREMOLATA

Combine ⅓ cup finely chopped
fresh flat-leaf parsley, 1 tablespoon
finely grated lemon rind and
2 cloves finely chopped garlic
in small bowl. Keep covered
in the fridge.

nutritional count per serving
0.1g total fat (0g saturated fat);
17kJ (4 cal); 0.3g carbohydrate;
0.2g protein; 0.6g fibre

prep time 10 minutes makes 1½ cups

VIETNAMESE CARROT PICKLE

Combine 1 crushed garlic clove,
1 finely chopped fresh long red chilli,
¼ cup lime juice, ¼ cup fish sauce,
¼ cup grated palm sugar, ½ cup water
and 1 coarsely grated medium carrot
in medium bowl; season to taste.

nutritional count per tablespoon 0g total fat
(0g saturated fat); 79kJ (19 cal);
4.1g carbohydrate; 0.4g protein; 0.3g fibre

prep + cook time 1 hour makes 3 cups

TOMATO KASAUNDI

Roughly chop 1 medium brown onion,
4 large tomatoes, 4 garlic cloves, 4 fresh
small red thai chillies; blend or process
with 2 tablespoons vegetable oil, ¼ cup
white vinegar, ⅓ cup firmly packed
light brown sugar, 2 teaspoons ground
cumin and ½ teaspoon each ground
turmeric and chilli powder, until
smooth. Transfer to large saucepan;
cook, stirring, without boiling, until
sugar dissolves. Simmer, uncovered,
stirring occasionally, about 45 minutes
or until kasaundi thickens slightly.

nutritional count per tablespoon 1.6g total
fat (0.2g saturated fat); 142kJ (34 cal);
4.1g carbohydrate; 0.5g protein; 0.6g fibre

prep + cook time 30 minutes **serves** 4

ROASTED CORN SALSA

Cook 2 trimmed corn cobs on heated oiled grill plate (or grill or barbecue) until browned all over. When cool enough to handle, cut kernels from cobs. Combine corn kernels in medium bowl with 1 coarsely chopped small red onion, 1 coarsely chopped large avocado, 250g (8 ounces) halved cherry tomatoes, 2 tablespoons lime juice and ¼ cup coarsely chopped fresh coriander (cilantro). Season to taste.

nutritional count per serving
14.5g total fat (2.9g saturated fat); 1200kJ (287 cal); 27.1g carbohydrate; 8 protein; 8.8g fibre

prep time 15 minutes **makes** 1 cup

MINT SAUCE

Blend or process 2 cups firmly packed fresh mint leaves and 2 quartered garlic cloves until smooth. With motor operating, gradually add ½ cup olive oil, in a thin, steady stream; blend until mixture is smooth. Stir in ¼ cup white wine vinegar and 1 tablespoon caster (superfine) sugar.

nutritional count per tablespoon 19g total fat (2.7g saturated fat); 748kJ (179 cal); 1.8g carbohydrate; 0.3g protein; 0.7g fibre

prep + cook time 10 minutes **makes** 2½ cups

CUCUMBER RAITA

Heat oil 2 teaspoons vegetable oil in small frying pan; cook ¼ teaspoon each black mustard seeds and cumin seeds, stirring, over low heat, 2 minutes or until seeds pop. Combine seeds with 500g (1 pound) yogurt, 2 seeded and finely chopped lebanese cucumbers and ¼ cup finely chopped fresh mint in medium bowl.

nutritional count per tablespoon 0.9g total fat (0.4g saturated fat); 63kJ (15 cal); 0.9g carbohydrate; 0.8g protein; 1.7g fibre

153

IN THE OVEN

middle-eastern chicken with fetta sauce (recipe page 158)

Sprinkle saffron threads over 2 tablespoons hot water in a small heatproof bowl; set aside.

Cut tops from the onions, peel away the brown skins, leaving the root ends intact. Trim root ends neatly.

Heat oil in flameproof dish, add onions, cover dish; cook, stirring occasionally, until onions are browned lightly.

prep + cook time 3 hours **serves** 4

middle-eastern chicken with fetta sauce

nutritional count per serving
52.6g total fat (17.2g saturated fat); 3457kJ (827 cal); 25.5g carbohydrate; 55.8g protein; 4.8g fibre
not suitable to freeze

(photograph page 157)

½ teaspoon saffron threads
2 tablespoons hot water
8 brown baby onions (200g)
2 tablespoons olive oil
4 cloves garlic, chopped finely
4 medium potatoes (800g), chopped coarsely
2 fresh long green chillies
1 teaspoon fennel seeds, ground coarsely
1½ teaspoons each ground cumin and coriander
4 medium tomatoes (600g), peeled, seeded, chopped coarsely
½ cup (125ml) dry white wine
1.8kg (3½-pound) chicken
2 tablespoons fresh coriander leaves (cilantro)

fetta sauce
125g (4 ounces) marinated fetta cheese, drained
1 teaspoon finely chopped preserved lemon rind
2 tablespoons finely chopped fresh coriander (cilantro)
¼ cup (60ml) water

Add the garlic, potato, chilli and spices to the dish; cook, stirring constantly for 1 minute to combine ingredients.

Add saffron mixture, tomato and wine to dish, bring to the boil, season, cover; cook in oven for 30 minutes.

Add chicken to dish, spoon juices over chicken, cover dish; cook in oven for 2 hours, or until chicken is tender.

Fetta sauce also makes an excellent accompaniment to slow-roasted lamb. To peel baby onions, pour boiling water over them in a heatproof bowl; stand 5 minutes, then the skins should just fall off.

1 Preheat oven to 125°C/250°F.
2 Soak saffron in the hot water in small heatproof bowl.
3 Meanwhile, peel onions, leaving root ends intact. Heat oil in 4-litre (16-cup) flameproof dish; cook onions, covered, stirring occasionally, over low heat until browned lightly. Add garlic, potato, chilli and spices; cook, stirring, 1 minute. Add saffron mixture, tomato and wine; bring to the boil, season. Cover; cook, in oven, 30 minutes.
4 Add chicken to dish; spoon some of the pan juices over chicken, cover; cook, in oven, 2 hours.
5 Meanwhile, make fetta sauce.
6 Discard chillies from dish. Serve chicken mixture drizzled with fetta sauce; sprinkle with coriander.

FETTA SAUCE
Blend or process ingredients until smooth; season to taste.

prep + cook time 2 hours 40 minutes serves 6

pork ragù with pappardelle

nutritional count per serving
17.3g total fat (5.9g saturated fat);
2475kJ (592 cal); 64.6g carbohydrate;
38.1g protein; 4.8g fibre
suitable to freeze at the end of step 4.
Cook pasta while reheating ragù. Sprinkle
with fennel fronds before serving.

2 x 5cm (2-inch) thick pork scotch steaks
  (750g)
2 tablespoons plain (all-purpose) flour
1 tablespoon olive oil
20g (¾ ounce) butter, chopped
1 medium leek (350g), sliced thinly
3 cloves garlic, sliced thinly
1 medium fennel bulb (200g), sliced thinly
½ cup (125ml) dry white wine
1½ cups (375ml) chicken stock
2 teaspoons balsamic vinegar
½ cup (80g) seeded green olives
500g (1 pound) pappardelle pasta
¼ cup coarsely chopped fennel fronds

1 Preheat oven to 160°C/325°F.
2 Toss pork in flour to coat; shake off excess. Heat oil and butter in flameproof
   baking dish; cook pork until browned all over. Remove from dish.
3 Cook leek, garlic and fennel in same dish, stirring, until softened. Add wine;
   bring to the boil. Reduce heat; simmer, uncovered, until wine is almost
   evaporated. Add stock; bring to the boil. Return pork to dish, cover with foil;
   cook in oven about 2 hours or until pork is tender, turning pork halfway
   through cooking time. Cool slightly, then shred the pork into small pieces.
4 Reheat the pork and sauce on stove top, stir in vinegar and olives.
5 Cook pasta in large saucepan of boiling water until tender; drain. Return to pan.
   Add pork and sauce to pasta; toss gently to combine. Season to taste.
6 Divide pasta into serving bowls, sprinkle with fennel fronds.

prep + cook time 3 hours 45 minutes serves 4

lamb rendang

nutritional count per serving
50.2g total fat (28.8g saturated fat);
3490kJ (835 cal); 8.1g carbohydrate;
86.5g protein; 3.7g fibre
serving suggestion Serve rendang with
steamed rice.
not suitable to freeze

2 teaspoons coriander seeds

¼ teaspoon ground turmeric

2 large brown onions (400g),
    chopped coarsely

4 cloves garlic, quartered

2 x 10cm (4-inch) sticks (40g) fresh
    lemon grass, chopped coarsely

2cm (¾-inch) piece fresh galangal (10g),
    sliced thinly

4 fresh small red thai (serrano) chillies,
    chopped coarsely

2 fresh long red chillies, chopped coarsely

2 tablespoons coarsely chopped coriander
    (cilantro) root and stem mixture

2 tablespoons peanut oil

1.5kg (3-pound) butterflied leg of lamb

1⅔ cups (410ml) coconut milk

We've given a spin to
a classic rendang, the
Malaysian meat curry that
is also eaten throughout
Indonesia and Singapore.
Traditionally slowly
cooked until the coconut
milk sauce thickens and
is quite dry, the succulent
meat becomes so tender
it virtually falls apart.

1 Dry-fry spices in small frying pan, stirring, about 1 minute or until fragrant.
    Blend or process spices with onion, garlic, lemon grass, galangal, chillies and
    coriander root and stem mixture until mixture forms a paste.
2 Preheat oven to 150°C/300°F.
3 Heat half the oil in large flameproof baking dish; cook lamb, turning occasionally,
    until browned all over. Remove from dish.
4 Heat remaining oil in same dish; cook paste, stirring, until fragrant. Add
    coconut milk; bring to the boil.
5 Return lamb to dish; cook in oven, uncovered, turning occasionally, about 3 hours
    or until liquid has evaporated. Cover lamb; stand 10 minutes before serving.
    Serve sprinkled with a little fresh coriander

prep + cook time 4 hours serves 4

confit of salmon with herb salad

nutritional count per serving
70.1g total fat (11.6g saturated fat);
3465kJ (829 cal); 7.2g carbohydrate;
40g protein; 4.8g fibre
tip You can use ocean trout instead of
the salmon.
serving suggestion Serve with steamed
baby new potatoes.
not suitable to freeze

1 large red capsicum (bell pepper) (350g)
2 baby fennel bulbs (260g), trimmed,
  halved, cored
2 small leeks (400g), white part only,
  halved lengthways
2 cloves garlic, bruised
1 fresh bay leaf
2 cups (500ml) light olive oil
1 cup (250ml) extra virgin olive oil
4 x 180g (5½-ounce) salmon fillets, skin on
¼ cup each firmly packed fresh dill sprigs,
  flat-leaf parsley, coriander (cilantro) and
    basil leaves
1 tablespoon lemon juice
1 tablespoon extra virgin olive oil, extra

dill mayonnaise
2 egg yolks
2 tablespoons lemon juice
1 teaspoon dijon mustard
¾ cup (180ml) light olive oil
2 tablespoons finely chopped fresh dill

Confit is a cooking term for foods that are preserved either by being salted and cooked slowly in their fat, or are cooked and preserved in oil in a similar method.

1 Preheat oven to 200°C/400°F.
2 Roast capsicum, uncovered, about 30 minutes or until skin blisters and blackens. Cover with paper or plastic; stand 5 minutes, then peel away skin. Discard seeds and membrane; slice capsicum thinly.
3 Reduce oven temperature to 125°C/250°F.
4 Place fennel and leek, cut-side down, in single layer in large baking dish. Add garlic and bay leaf; pour over combined oils. Cover with baking paper; bake about 1 hour or until vegetables are tender. Remove vegetables from dish; drain on absorbent paper.
5 Reduce oven temperature to 50°C/100°F.
6 Place salmon, skin-side down, in oil in dish; cover with baking paper. Bake about 2½ hours or until salmon is heated through, but still looks glassy. Remove salmon; drain on absorbent paper.
7 Meanwhile, make dill mayonnaise.
8 Combine herbs, juice and extra oil in medium bowl; season to taste.
9 Serve salmon topped with vegetables, herb salad and dill mayonnaise.

DILL MAYONNAISE
Blend egg yolks, juice and mustard until smooth. With motor operating, gradually add oil in a thin, steady stream; blend until mayonnaise is thick. Stir in dill; season to taste. Add a little boiling water if mayonnaise is too thick.

prep + cook time 3 hours (+ standing) serves 8

chicken cassoulet

nutritional count per serving
41.8g total fat (14.1g saturated fat);
3026kJ (724 cal); 16.5g carbohydrate;
64.9g protein; 7.6g fibre
suitable to freeze Cook bacon and
sprinkle over cassoulet after reheating.

1 cup (200g) dried haricot beans
500g (1 pound) spicy italian sausages
250g (8 ounces) pork sausages
4 chicken thighs (900g)
4 chicken breasts on the bone (1kg)
1 tablespoon vegetable oil
3 rindless bacon slices (195g), sliced thinly
2 cloves garlic, crushed
3 cloves

12 black peppercorns
1 stalk celery (150g), trimmed,
   chopped coarsely
4 medium carrots (480g), sliced thinly
5 baby onions (125g), halved
½ cup (125ml) dry white wine
3 cups (750ml) water
2 tablespoons tomato paste
¼ cup fresh flat-leaf parsley, finely chopped

1 Place beans in large bowl, cover with water. Stand overnight; drain. Rinse
  under cold water; drain.
2 Preheat oven to 180°C/350°F.
3 Cook sausages in large saucepan of boiling water, uncovered, 2 minutes; drain.
4 Remove skin from chicken; cut breasts in half.
5 Heat oil in 5-litre (20-cup) flameproof casserole dish; cook chicken and sausages,
  in batches, until browned. Drain on absorbent paper; slice sausages thickly.
6 Add bacon to dish; cook, stirring, until crisp. Drain on absorbent paper.
7 Return chicken to dish with beans, garlic, spices, vegetables, wine, the water
  and tomato paste. Cook, covered, in oven 1½ hours.
8 Add sausages; cover. Cook about 30 minutes or until sausages are cooked.
  Season to taste. Serve sprinkled with bacon and parsley.

prep + cook time 2 hours 20 minutes
(+ refrigeration) **serves** 8

sticky glazed
slow-roast
pork

½ cup (125ml) chinese cooking wine
   (shao hsing) or medium dry sherry
½ cup (125ml) dark soy sauce
⅓ cup (75g) firmly packed light brown sugar
4 cloves garlic, crushed
5cm (2-inch) piece fresh ginger (25g), grated
1 teaspoon sesame oil
2 star anise
2 x 1kg (2-pound) pieces pork neck
1½ cups (375ml) water

1   Combine cooking wine, soy sauce, sugar, garlic, ginger, oil and star anise
    in medium jug. Reserve half the soy mixture in separate jug; refrigerate,
    covered, until ready to serve.
2   Place pork in large baking dish. Pour remaining soy mixture over pork; turn
    to coat pork in mixture. Cover; refrigerate 3 hours, turning pork occasionally.
3   Preheat oven to 160°C/325°F.
4   Lift pork onto a wire rack in same baking dish. Pour the water into dish.
    Roast pork, uncovered, about 2 hours, brushing occasionally with pan juices.
    Remove pork from dish; cover with foil, stand 15 minutes before slicing.
5   Serve pork sliced, drizzled with reserved soy mixture.

nutritional count per serving 8.6g total fat (3.1g saturated fat); 1421kJ (340 cal);
9.8g carbohydrate; 51.9g protein; 0.3g fibre
not suitable to freeze

prep + cook time 2 hours 45 minutes
serves 6

slow-roasted beef shanks

1 Preheat oven to 180°C/350°F.
2 Toss shank pieces in flour to coat; shake off excess. Heat oil in large frying pan; cook shank pieces, in batches, until browned and almost crunchy all over.
3 Place undrained tomatoes, wine, stock and paste in deep 5-litre (20-cup) baking dish; stir to combine. Place shank pieces, one at a time, standing upright, in dish; roast, covered, about 2 hours or until tender.
4 Remove shanks from dish. When cool enough to handle, remove meat from bones. Discard bones; chop meat coarsely. Return meat to dish with tomato sauce; reheat if necessary. Season to taste. Stir in herbs just before serving.

nutritional count per serving 18.8g total fat (6.1g saturated fat); 1701kJ (407 cal); 8.5g carbohydrate; 46.4g protein; 2.4g fibre
tip Ask your butcher to quarter the beef shank crossways so that the pieces will fit into the baking dish.
suitable to freeze Stir in herbs after reheating.

1 large beef shank (2.5kg), quartered crossways
2 tablespoons plain (all-purpose) flour
2 tablespoons olive oil
800g (1½ pounds) canned crushed tomatoes
½ cup (125ml) dry white wine
½ cup (125ml) beef stock
¼ cup (70g) tomato paste
¼ cup finely chopped fresh flat-leaf parsley
2 tablespoons finely chopped fresh lemon thyme

169

prep + cook time 5 hours 10 minutes (+ standing) **serves** 10

slow-roasted turkey with wild rice seasoning

nutritional count per serving
44.4g total fat (19.6g saturated fat);
2947kJ (705 cal); 25.2g carbohydrate;
47.4g protein; 1.7g fibre
serving suggestion Serve with steamed
green beans and baby carrots.
not suitable to freeze

4kg (8-pound) whole turkey
90g (3 ounces) butter, melted
1 litre (4 cups) water
45g (1½ ounces) butter, extra
¼ cup (35g) plain (all-purpose) flour
⅓ cup (80ml) port
2 cups (500ml) chicken stock

wild rice seasoning
45g (1½ ounces) butter
1 large brown onion (200g),
   chopped coarsely
2 cloves garlic, crushed
⅓ cup (60g) wild rice
½ cup (125ml) dry white wine
1 cup (250ml) water
⅔ cup (130g) basmati rice
2 cups (500ml) chicken stock
2 medium zucchini (240g), grated coarsely
2 teaspoons finely grated lemon rind
2 teaspoons lemon thyme leaves
1 cup (70g) stale breadcrumbs

1   Make wild rice seasoning.
2   Preheat oven to 150°C/300°F.
3   Discard neck from turkey. Rinse turkey under cold water, pat dry inside and out. Fill neck cavity with seasoning; secure skin over opening with toothpicks. Fill large cavity with seasoning; tie legs together with kitchen string, tuck wing tips under turkey. Place turkey on oiled wire rack in flameproof baking dish.
4   Dip 50cm (20-inch) piece of muslin into the melted butter and place over turkey. Add the water to baking dish, cover with foil. Roast 4 hours.
5   Remove foil and muslin from turkey, brush with pan juices. Increase oven to 200°C/400°F; roast 30 minutes or until turkey is cooked. Remove from oven; cover, stand 20 minutes. Drain pan juices into large jug; skim fat from top of juices, discard. You will need about 2 cups of pan juices.
6   Place same baking dish over medium heat on stove top; melt butter, add flour. Cook, stirring, until well browned. Gradually stir in port, reserved juices and stock; cook, stirring, until mixture boils and thickens. Strain into large jug.
7   Serve turkey and seasoning with gravy.

WILD RICE SEASONING
Heat butter in large frying pan; cook onion and garlic, stirring, until onion is soft. Add wild rice; cook, stirring, 1 minute. Add wine; simmer, covered, 10 minutes or until almost all the liquid is absorbed. Add the water; simmer, covered, about 10 minutes or until liquid is absorbed. Add basmati rice; cook, stirring, 1 minute. Add stock; simmer, covered, 10 minutes or until liquid is absorbed and rice is tender. Stir in zucchini, rind and thyme; cool. Add breadcrumbs; mix well.

prep + cook time 3 hours 30 minutes **serves** 4

moroccan-spiced lamb shoulder

nutritional count per serving
21.9g total fat (7.3g saturated fat);
1722kJ (412 cal); 6.5g carbohydrate;
45.7g protein; 3.1g fibre
serving suggestion Serve with steamed
green beans and baked potatoes.
not suitable to freeze

2 teaspoons fennel seeds

1 teaspoon each ground cinnamon,
ginger and cumin

¼ teaspoon chilli powder

2 tablespoons olive oil

1.2kg (2½-pound) lamb shoulder,
shank intact

2 cloves garlic, sliced thinly

6 baby brown onions (150g)

375g (12 ounces) baby carrots, trimmed

1 cup (250ml) water

1 Preheat oven to 180°C/350°F.

2 Dry-fry spices in small frying pan until fragrant. Combine spices and half the oil in small bowl.

3 Using sharp knife, score lamb at 2.5cm (1-inch) intervals; push garlic into cuts. Rub lamb all over with spice mixture, season.

4 Heat remaining oil in large flameproof dish; cook lamb, turning, until browned all over. Remove lamb from dish.

5 Meanwhile, peel onions, leaving root ends intact. Add onions to dish; cook, stirring, until browned.

6 Add carrots and the water to dish, bring to the boil; top with lamb, cover loosely with foil. Transfer to oven; roast 1½ hours.

7 Reduce oven temperature to 160°C/325°F.

8 Uncover lamb; roast a further 1½ hours or until lamb is tender. Cover lamb; stand 10 minutes, then slice thinly. Strain pan juices into small heatproof jug.

9 Serve lamb with onions, carrots and pan juices.

prep + cook time 1 hour 20 minutes (+ standing) **serves** 6

leek, bean and mushroom bake

nutritional count per serving
3.7g total fat (0.5g saturated fat);
949kJ (227 cal); 28.6g carbohydrate;
11.4g protein; 11g fibre
tip We used dried cannellini beans, but
any white beans, such as northern, navy
or haricot beans, will be fine.
not suitable to freeze

1 cup (200g) dried white beans
2 teaspoons olive oil
2 medium leeks (700g), sliced thinly
3 cloves garlic, crushed
350g (11 ounces) swiss brown mushrooms,
 halved
2 stalks celery (300g), trimmed,
 chopped coarsely

½ cup (125ml) dry red wine
1 cup (250ml) vegetable stock
700g (1½ pounds) bottled tomato pasta
 sauce (passata)
3 sprigs fresh thyme
1 cup (120g) frozen peas
3 slices multigrain bread (135g),
 toasted, halved

1 Place beans in medium bowl, cover with water. Stand overnight, drain; rinse under cold water, drain. Cook beans in medium saucepan of boiling water about 20 minutes or until tender; drain.
2 Preheat oven to 200°C/400°F.
3 Heat oil in large flameproof baking dish; cook leek, garlic, mushrooms and celery, stirring, until vegetables soften. Add wine; bring to the boil. Boil, uncovered, until liquid is reduced by half. Add beans, stock, sauce and thyme; bring to the boil.
4 Cover dish, transfer to oven; bake 30 minutes. Stir in peas; bake, uncovered, about 20 minutes or until sauce thickens slightly. Season to taste; sprinkle with extra thyme. Serve bake with toast.

prep + cook time 3 hours 30 minutes serves 6

braised lamb shanks with tzatziki and tomato salad

nutritional count per serving
37.1g total fat (11.5g saturated fat);
2834kJ (678 cal); 33.5g carbohydrate;
41.6g protein; 9.5g fibre
tips Remove lamb from the bone; add
a little more stock to the mixture and
serve as a thick soup.
serving suggestion Serve with warmed or
grilled pitta bread to mop up the juices.
suitable to freeze at the end of step 3.

⅓ cup (80ml) light olive oil
6 french-trimmed lamb shanks (1.5kg)
1 large brown onion (200g), chopped finely
1 large carrot (180g), chopped coarsely
1 stalk celery (150g), trimmed,
    chopped finely
4 cloves garlic, chopped finely
2 cups (500ml) chicken stock
1 cup (250ml) dry white wine
2 tablespoons tomato paste
½ cup (100g) pearl barley
½ cup (100g) dried brown lentils
400g (12½ ounces) canned chickpeas
    (garbanzo beans), rinsed, drained
4 sprigs fresh thyme

1 cup (250ml) water
4 medium egg (plum) tomatoes (300g),
    chopped coarsely
1 tablespoon lemon juice
2 tablespoons extra virgin olive oil
⅓ cup finely chopped fresh flat-leaf parsley
tzatziki
1 lebanese cucumber (130g), peeled,
    seeded, grated finely
1 cup (280g) yogurt
1 tablespoon lemon juice
2 cloves garlic, crushed
2 tablespoons finely chopped fresh mint

1 Preheat oven to 125°C/250°F.
2 Heat light olive oil in 6-litre (24-cup) flameproof dish; cook lamb, in batches, until browned all over. Remove from dish.
3 Add onion, carrot and celery to same dish; cook, covered, over low heat, stirring occasionally, until soft. Add garlic, stock, wine, paste, barley, lentils, chickpeas and thyme; bring to the boil. Return lamb to dish, cover; cook, in oven, 2 hours. Stir in the water; cook, in oven, covered, about 1 hour or until lamb is almost falling off the bone. Season to taste.
4 Meanwhile combine tomato, juice, extra virgin olive oil and half the parsley in small bowl; season to taste.
5 Make tzatziki.
6 Sprinkle lamb with remaining parsley; serve with tomato salad and tzatziki.

TZATZIKI
Squeeze excess liquid from cucumber; combine cucumber with remaining ingredients in small bowl. Season to taste.

prep + cook time 4 hours 15 minutes **serves** 6

braised rabbit sauce with fettuccine

nutritional count per serving
25g total fat (5.2g saturated fat);
3164kJ (757 cal); 83.3g carbohydrate;
38g protein; 7.6g fibre
tips Other types of pasta, such as penne,
also work well.
suitable to freeze at the end of step 4.

⅓ cup (80ml) light olive oil
900g (1¾-pound) rabbit, cut into 8 pieces
1 medium red onion (170g), chopped finely
2 medium carrots (240g), chopped finely
1 medium parsnip (250g), chopped finely
1 stalk celery (150g), trimmed,
  chopped finely
8 cloves garlic, chopped finely
800g (1½ pounds) canned crushed
  tomatoes

2 tablespoons tomato paste
1 cup (250ml) chicken stock
1 cup (250ml) dry red wine
2 teaspoons dried rigani
1 sprig fresh rosemary
1 cinnamon stick
600g (1¼ pounds) fettuccine pasta
2 tablespoons extra virgin olive oil
½ cup (40g) finely grated pecorino cheese

1 Preheat oven to 125°C/250°F.
2 Heat half the light olive oil in 6-litre (24-cup) flameproof dish; cook rabbit, in batches, until browned. Remove from dish.
3 Heat remaining light olive oil in same dish; cook onion, carrot, parsnip and celery, covered, stirring occasionally, over low heat until soft. Add garlic, undrained tomatoes, paste, stock, wine, herbs and cinnamon; bring to the boil. Return rabbit to dish, cover; cook, in oven, about 3½ hours or until rabbit is falling off the bone.
4 Remove rabbit from dish. When cool enough to handle, remove meat from bones; discard bones. Return meat to dish; season to taste. Cook, stirring, until hot.
5 Meanwhile, cook pasta in large saucepan of boiling water until tender; drain. Toss pasta with extra virgin oil; season to taste.
6 Serve pasta topped with sauce; sprinkle with cheese.

prep + cook time 5 hours 30 minutes serves 4

sweet and sour lamb with burghul salad

nutritional count per serving
54.4g total fat (14.1g saturated fat);
4059kJ (971 cal); 36.7g carbohydrate;
78.8g protein; 9g fibre
not suitable to freeze

2 teaspoons each finely chopped fresh
   thyme, coriander (cilantro) and rosemary
4 cloves garlic
1 teaspoon sea salt flakes
½ teaspoon black peppercorns
2 tablespoons light olive oil
1.4kg (2¾-pound) boned lamb shoulder
½ cup (125ml) chicken stock
½ cup (125ml) cider vinegar
1 teaspoon dijon mustard
2 tablespoons roasted slivered almonds

burghul salad
1 tablespoon light olive oil
2 green onions (scallions), chopped finely
1 cup (160g) burghul
1½ cups (375ml) chicken stock
¼ cup each finely chopped fresh mint,
   flat-leaf parsley, basil and oregano
1 tablespoon finely chopped preserved
   lemon rind
4 dried apricots (35g), chopped finely
4 fresh dates (80g), seeded, chopped
   finely
1 tablespoon toasted sesame seeds
2 tablespoons roasted slivered almonds
¼ cup (60ml) lemon-infused olive oil

1 Preheat oven to 125°C/250°F.
2 Blend or process herbs, garlic, salt, pepper and oil until combined.
3 Rub herb mixture all over lamb; place lamb in 2-litre (8-cup) flameproof dish.
   Bring stock, vinegar and mustard to the boil in small saucepan; pour mixture
   around lamb, cover. Cook, in oven, 4 hours.
4 Uncover lamb; cook, in oven, 1 hour.
5 Meanwhile, make burghul salad.
6 Serve lamb and pan juices with burghul salad; sprinkle with nuts.

BURGHUL SALAD
Heat oil in medium saucepan; cook onion, stirring, until soft, stir in burghul.
Add stock; bring to the boil, season. Cover; cook, over low heat, about
10 minutes or until liquid is absorbed. Transfer to medium bowl; fluff
with fork, cool. Stir in remaining ingredients; season to taste.

prep + cook time 4 hours 15 minutes (+ refrigeration) serves 6

beef cheeks with mushrooms and braised cabbage

nutritional count per serving
33.5g total fat (9.1g saturated fat);
3093kJ (740 cal); 19.1g carbohydrate;
63.2g protein; 7.8g fibre
serving suggestions Serve with mashed
sweet potato or cannellini beans.
suitable to freeze at the end of step 5.

4 beef cheeks (1.6kg)
1 medium brown onion (150g),
  chopped coarsely
1 medium carrot (120g), chopped coarsely
1 stalk celery (150g), trimmed,
  chopped coarsely
8 cloves garlic, bruised
1 dried bay leaf
6 sprigs fresh flat-leaf parsley
2 cups (500ml) dry red wine
1 cup (250ml) tawny port
¼ cup (35g) plain (all-purpose) flour

⅓ cup (80ml) olive oil
2 cups (500ml) beef stock
1 tablespoon dried porcini mushrooms,
  chopped coarsely
2 tablespoons tomato paste
8 large portobello mushrooms (400g),
  trimmed
braised cabbage
2 tablespoons olive oil
1 medium red onion (170g), sliced thinly
½ small savoy cabbage (600g),
  shredded finely

1 Combine beef with vegetables, garlic, bay leaf, parsley, wine and port in large bowl, cover; refrigerate overnight.
2 Preheat oven to 110°C/220°F.
3 Drain beef and vegetables, reserve marinade. Pat beef and vegetables dry with absorbent paper. Toss beef in flour to coat; shake off excess.
4 Heat half the oil in 6-litre (24-cup) flameproof dish; cook beef, in batches, until browned. Remove from dish.
5 Add vegetables to dish; cook, stirring, until browned lightly. Add reserved marinade, stock, dried mushrooms and paste; bring to the boil. Return beef to dish, season, cover; cook, in oven, 3½ hours.
6 Heat remaining oil in large frying pan; cook portobello mushrooms, stirring occasionally, until browned lightly. Transfer to another ovenproof dish, cover; cook, in oven, for the last 1 hour of beef cooking time.
7 Meanwhile, make braised cabbage.
8 Remove beef and mushrooms from dishes; cover to keep warm. Strain cooking liquid into large heatproof jug; return to pan. Bring to the boil; boil, uncovered, until reduced by half.
9 Slice beef cheeks; serve topped with mushrooms and sauce, accompany with braised cabbage.

BRAISED CABBAGE
Heat oil in large saucepan; cook onion, stirring, until softened. Add cabbage, stir to combine; cook, covered, over low heat, stirring occasionally, about 5 minutes or until cabbage is tender. Season to taste.

prep + cook time 3 hours 40 minutes serves 6

duck legs with pancetta and white beans

nutritional count per serving
80.5g total fat (23g saturated fat);
3938kJ (942 cal); 14.6g carbohydrate;
33.7g protein; 3.9g fibre
tips If breadcrumbs are not brown, place
dish under hot grill for a few seconds until
crisp. We used cannellini beans, but you
can use any white bean you like.
serving suggestion Serve with steamed
green beans or wilted spinach.
not suitable to freeze

⅓ cup (80ml) light olive oil
200g (6½ ounces) thinly sliced pancetta,
  chopped coarsely
1 large brown onion (200g),
  chopped finely
2 medium carrots (240g), chopped finely
1 stalk celery (150g), trimmed,
  chopped finely

6 sprigs fresh thyme
6 duck marylands (1.8kg)
1 cup (250ml) dry red wine
1 cup (250ml) chicken stock
800g (1½ pounds) canned white beans,
  rinsed, drained
1 cup (70g) stale breadcrumbs

Duck marylands have
the leg and thigh still
connected in a single
piece; the bones and
skin remain intact.

1 Preheat oven to 110°C/220°F.
2 Heat half the oil in large frying pan; cook pancetta, stirring, until crisp.
   Remove pancetta from pan, place in large baking dish.
3 Heat remaining oil in same pan; cook onion, carrot, celery and thyme,
   stirring, until soft. Transfer to dish; top with duck.
4 Bring wine and stock to the boil in small saucepan; pour over duck. Cover
   dish with foil; roast, in oven, 2 hours. Remove from oven.
5 Increase oven temperature to 125°C/250°F.
6 Remove foil; stir beans into dish, sprinkle duck with breadcrumbs. Roast,
   uncovered, about 1 hour or until duck is tender.
7 Serve duck, vegetables and pan juices on bed of wilted spinach.

prep + cook time 6 hours 20 minutes serves 6

leg of lamb with couscous and eggplant puree

nutritional count per serving
20.1g total fat (6.2g saturated fat);
2270kJ (543 cal); 36.6g carbohydrate;
44.1g protein; 5.5g fibre
not suitable to freeze

2kg (4-pound) leg of lamb, shank removed
2 cloves garlic, sliced thinly
4 sprigs fresh rosemary
3 medium zucchini (360g), halved
  lengthways
3 medium carrots (360g), halved
  lengthways
1 medium (200g) red capsicum
  (bell pepper), chopped coarsely
1 cup (250ml) chicken stock
1 cup (250ml) dry white wine
1 cup (200g) israeli (pearl) couscous
½ cup (80g) seeded green olives

eggplant puree
1 large eggplant (500g)
½ teaspoon ground cumin
2 cloves garlic, chopped finely
2 tablespoons lemon juice
¼ cup (60ml) extra virgin olive oil

Israeli couscous, also known as pearl couscous, is made of baked wheat rather than semolina (like the couscous from North Africa). Its granules are much larger (its size and shape is similar to a pearl) and it maintains its texture and firmness without sticking. It is available from most major supermarkets.

1   Preheat oven to 125°C/250°F.
2   Make small incisions in lamb; push garlic and leaves from 2 sprigs of the rosemary into cuts.
3   Place remaining rosemary in large baking dish; top with lamb, season. Tuck zucchini, carrot and capsicum around lamb. Bring combined stock and wine to the boil in small saucepan; pour around lamb. Cover dish with foil; roast 5½ hours.
4   Meanwhile, make eggplant puree.
5   Remove foil from baking dish; stir in couscous and olives. Cover; roast about 30 minutes or until couscous is tender and lamb is falling off the bone. Season to taste.
6   Serve lamb with vegetables, pan juices and eggplant puree.

EGGPLANT PUREE
Cut eggplant in half lengthways; score flesh. Place eggplant, cut-sides up on oven tray; sprinkle with cumin. Roast, uncovered, alongside lamb, about 2½ hours or until eggplant is soft. When cool enough to handle, scoop out flesh, discard skins. Blend or process eggplant with remaining ingredients until smooth. Season to taste.

prep + cook time 3 hours 45 minutes (+ standing) serves 4

twice-cooked asian pork belly with steamed ginger rice

nutritional count per serving
24.8g total fat (6.4g saturated fat);
3005kJ (719 cal); 62.7g carbohydrate;
60.1g protein; 1.1g fibre
tips Pork can be poached and weighted
a day in advance; keep covered in the
refrigerator. If skin is not crisp, place
under hot grill for a few seconds.
serving suggestions Serve with steamed
or stir-fried asian greens.
not suitable to freeze

1kg (2-pound) pork belly, rind on
2 star anise
1 cinnamon stick
1 tablespoon olive oil
1 teaspoon five-spice powder
1 teaspoon coarse cooking salt (kosher salt)
¼ cup (60ml) japanese soy sauce
2 tablespoons lemon juice
2 teaspoons sesame oil
2 tablespoons each fresh coriander
   (cilantro) and mint leaves

steamed ginger rice
1 tablespoon olive oil
6 green onions (scallions), sliced thinly
2.5cm (1-inch) piece fresh ginger (15g),
   grated
1½ cups (300g) basmati rice
2 cups (500ml) chicken stock
2 tablespoons each finely chopped fresh
   coriander (cilantro) and mint

1 Using a sharp knife, score pork rind at 1cm (½-inch) intervals. Place pork in
   large saucepan with star anise and cinnamon; cover with cold water. Bring to
   the boil, skimming scum from surface. Reduce heat; simmer gently, covered
   loosely, about 1 hour.
2 Drain pork; place on oven tray, top with baking paper and another tray. Weight
   with heavy cans; stand about 2 hours or until pork is uniform in thickness.
3 Preheat oven to 220°C/425°F.
4 Combine olive oil, five-spice and salt in small bowl; rub all over pork rind.
   Place pork on wire rack over large baking dish; pour enough water into dish
   to come 2cm (¾ inch) up sides of dish without touching pork. Roast pork,
   uncovered, 30 minutes.
5 Reduce oven temperature to 125°C/250°F; roast pork, uncovered, about 2 hours
   or until tender and crackling is crisp.
6 Meanwhile, make steamed ginger rice.
7 Combine sauce, juice and sesame oil in small bowl.
8 Cut pork into 12 pieces; serve with rice, drizzle with soy dressing, sprinkle
   with herbs.

STEAMED GINGER RICE
Heat oil in medium saucepan; cook onion, stirring, until softened. Add ginger
and rice; stir to coat in oil. Add stock; bring to the boil. Reduce heat; simmer,
covered, over low heat, 10 minutes. Remove from heat; stand, covered, 5 minutes.
Fluff rice with fork; stir in herbs, season to taste.

prep + cook time 4 hours serves 6

pot-roast beef with anchovies, chilli and soft polenta

nutritional count per serving
32.5g total fat (13.3g saturated fat);
2980kJ (713 cal); 31.9g carbohydrate;
68.6g protein; 2.4g fibre
serving suggestions Serve with steamed
green beans or wilted spinach.
not suitable to freeze

2 tablespoons olive oil
1.5kg (3-pound) corner piece beef rump
10 shallots (250g)
2 fresh small red thai (serrano) chillies,
 chopped finely
8 drained anchovy fillets, chopped finely
200g (6½ ounces) italian-style pork
 sausages
½ cup (125ml) dry red wine
400g (12½ ounces) canned diced
 tomatoes

soft polenta
1 litre (4 cups) milk
1 litre (4 cups) water
1 medium brown onion (150g), quartered
2 dried bay leaves
1 cup (170g) polenta

1 Preheat oven to 125°C/250°F.
2 Heat oil in 6-litre (24-cup) flameproof dish; cook beef, turning, until browned
   all over. Remove from dish.
3 Meanwhile, peel shallots, leaving root ends intact. Add to same dish; cook,
   stirring, until browned lightly. Add chilli and anchovies; squeeze sausage
   meat from casings into dish. Cook, stirring, until anchovies are soft and
   sausage meat is browned.
4 Add wine and undrained tomatoes; bring to the boil. Return beef to pan,
   season, cover; cook, in oven, 3 hours.
5 Make soft polenta.
6 Remove beef from dish; cover to keep warm. Strain sauce through fine
   sieve into large heatproof jug; reserve sausage mixture. Return sauce to
   dish; bring to the boil. Boil, uncovered, until reduced by half. Return sausage
   mixture to sauce.
7 Serve sliced beef with sauce and soft polenta.

SOFT POLENTA
Combine milk, the water, onion and bay leaves in large saucepan; bring to
the boil. Remove from heat; stand 10 minutes. Discard onion and bay leaves.
Slowly whisk polenta into milk mixture; cook, stirring, over low heat, about
30 minutes or until polenta is soft. Season to taste.

Accompaniments
VEGETABLES

prep + cook time 25 minutes **serves** 6

STEAMED GAI LAN IN OYSTER SAUCE

Boil, steam or microwave 1kg (2 pounds) gai lan until just tender; drain. Heat 1 tablespoon peanut oil in wok; stir-fry gai lan, 1 tablespoon japanese soy sauce and 2 tablespoons oyster sauce, about 2 minutes or until gai lan is tender.

nutritional count per serving
3.4g total fat (0.6g saturated fat); 226kJ (54 cal); 2.6g carbohydrate; 2.1g protein; 2.2g fibre

prep + cook time 40 minutes **serves** 6

FRESH PEAS, CARAWAY AND PARMESAN

Melt 60g (2 ounces) butter in large frying pan; cook 1 teaspoon caraway seeds, 2 teaspoons finely grated lemon rind and 1 thinly sliced small red onion, stirring, until onion softens. Add 4 cups shelled fresh peas; cook, stirring, until peas are just tender. Stir in ⅓ cup coarsely chopped fresh flat-leaf parsley; sprinkle with ½ cup finely grated parmesan cheese.

nutritional count per serving 8.1g total fat (5.1g saturated fat); 598kJ (143 cal); 8.5g carbohydrate; 6.8g protein; 4.8g fibre

tip You need about 1.3kg fresh peas to get the amount of podded peas required for this recipe.

prep + cook time 35 minutes **serves** 6

TOMATO-BRAISED BEANS

Heat 1 tablespoon olive oil in large saucepan; cook 1 coarsely chopped medium brown onion and 2 crushed garlic cloves, stirring, until onion softens. Add 1kg (2 pounds) trimmed green beans and 4 coarsely chopped medium tomatoes; cook, covered, stirring occasionally, about 20 minutes or until vegetables soften slightly. Season to taste.

nutritional count per serving 3.5g total fat (0.4g saturated fat); 397kJ (95 cal); 7.4g carbohydrate; 5.1g protein; 6.2g fibre

prep + cook time 35 minutes **serves** 4

CELERIAC PUREE

Bring 2 cups chicken stock to the boil in medium saucepan; add 1kg (2 pounds) coarsely chopped celeriac (celery root), return to the boil. Reduce heat; simmer, covered, about 30 minutes or until celeriac is tender. Drain. Blend or process celeriac, in batches, with ½ cup pouring cream until smooth. Season to taste; serve sprinkled with 1 tablespoon finely chopped fresh chives.

nutritional count per serving
14.4g total fat (9.2g saturated fat); 815kJ (195 cal); 7.4g carbohydrate; 5.2g protein; 8.8g fibre

prep + cook time 15 minutes **serves** 4

CREAMED SPINACH

Melt 20g (¾ ounce) butter in large frying pan; cook 600g (1¼ pounds) spinach, stirring, until wilted. Add ½ cup pouring cream; bring to the boil. Reduce heat; simmer, uncovered, until liquid reduces by half. Blend or process mixture until smooth; season to taste.

nutritional count per serving 38.7g total fat (25.4g saturated fat); 1555kJ (372 cal); 2.8g carbohydrate; 3.5g protein; 2.1g fibre

prep + cook time 1 hour 10 minutes **serves** 4

ROASTED CARAMELISED PARSNIPS

Preheat oven to 220°C/425°F. Halve 1kg (2 pounds) parsnips lengthways. Combine parsnip with 2 tablespoons olive oil, ¼ cup firmly packed light brown sugar and 1 teaspoon ground nutmeg in large baking dish, season; roast about 1 hour or until parsnip is browned and tender. Serve parsnip sprinkled with 1 tablespoon finely chopped fresh flat-leaf parsley.

nutritional count per serving 9.6g total fat (1.3g saturated fat); 1074kJ (257 cal); 35.8g carbohydrate; 4.1g protein; 5.7g fibre

Glossary

ALLSPICE also known as pimento or jamaican pepper; available whole or ground. Tastes like a blend of cinnamon, clove and nutmeg – all spices.

BEANS

black turtle also known as black or black kidney beans; an earthy-flavoured dried bean completely different from the better-known chinese black beans (which are fermented soya beans).

cannellini small white bean that is similar in appearance and flavour to haricot, great northern and navy beans, all of which can be substituted for the other.

kidney medium-sized red bean, slightly floury in texture, yet sweet in flavour.

snake long (about 40cm/16 inches), thin, round, fresh green bean; Asian in origin with a taste similar to green beans. Are also known as yard-long beans because of their (pre-metric) length.

BEEF

blade from the shoulder; isn't as tender as other cuts, so it needs slow-roasting.

brisket a cheaper cut from the belly; available with or without bones as a joint for slow-roasting, or for stewing and casseroling as cubes or mince.

cheeks the cheek muscle. A very tough and lean cut of meat; often used for braising or slow cooking to produce a tender result.

chuck from the neck and shoulder of the beef; tends to be chewy but flavourful and inexpensive. A good cut for stewing or braising.

corned silverside also known as topside roast; sold vacuum-sealed in brine.

gravy beef also known as beef shin or shank, cut from the lower shin.

osso buco literally meaning 'bone with a hole', osso buco is cut from the shin of the hind leg. It is also known as knuckle.

sausages seasoned and spiced minced (ground) beef mixed with cereal and packed into casings. Also known as snags or bangers.

shank, see gravy beef, above.

short ribs cut from the rib section; usually larger, more tender and meatier than pork spare ribs.

BEETROOT also known as red beets or beets; firm, round root vegetable.

BICARBONATE OF SODA also known as baking or carb soda; a leavening agent.

BREADCRUMBS, STALE one- or two-day-old bread made into crumbs by grating, blending or processing.

BUK CHOY also known as bok choy, pak choi, chinese white cabbage or chinese chard; has a fresh, mild mustard taste.

BUTTER use salted or unsalted (sweet) butter; 125g equals one stick (4 ounces).

CAPERS grey-green buds of a warm climate (usually Mediterranean) shrub, sold either dried and salted or pickled in a vinegar brine. Capers must be rinsed well before using.

CAPSICUM also known as bell pepper or pepper. Comes in many colours: red, green, yellow, orange and purplish-black. Be sure to discard seeds and membranes before use.

CAVOLO NERO, or tuscan cabbage, is a staple in Tuscan country cooking. It has long, narrow, wrinkled leaves and a rich and astringent, mild cabbage flavour. It doesn't lose its volume like silver beet or spinach when cooked, but it does need longer cooking.

CHICKEN

drumsticks leg with skin and bone intact.

thigh cutlets thigh with skin and centre bone intact; sometimes found skinned with bone intact.

thigh fillets the skin and bone removed.

CHILLI available in many types and sizes. Use rubber gloves when seeding and chopping fresh chillies as they can burn your skin. Removing membranes and seeds lessens the heat level.

cayenne pepper dried, long, thin-fleshed, extremely hot, ground red chilli.

flakes dried, deep-red, dehydrated chilli slices and whole seeds.

long green any unripened chilli.

long red available both fresh and dried; a generic term used for any moderately hot, thin, long (6-8cm/2¼-3¼ inch) chilli.

powder can be used as a substitute for fresh chillies (½ teaspoon ground chilli powder to 1 chopped medium fresh chilli).

CHINESE COOKING WINE also known as shao hsing or chinese rice wine; made from fermented rice, wheat, sugar and salt. Found in Asian food shops; if you can't find it, replace with mirin or sherry.

CHORIZO SAUSAGES a sausage of Spanish origin, made from coarsely ground smoked pork and highly seasoned with garlic, chilli powder and other spices.

CORIANDER also known as pak chee, cilantro or chinese parsley; bright-green-leafed herb with a pungent flavour. The leaves, stems and roots of coriander are also used. Wash under cold water, removing any dirt clinging to the roots; scrape the roots with a small flat knife to remove some of the outer fibrous skin. Chop roots and stems together to obtain the amount specified. Also available ground or as seeds; these should not be substituted for fresh coriander as the tastes are completely different.

COUSCOUS a fine, dehydrated, grain-like cereal product made from semolina; it swells to three or four times its original size when liquid is added.

CRANBERRIES, DRIED have the same slightly sour, succulent flavour as fresh cranberries. Available in supermarkets.

CREAM we use fresh cream, also known as pure cream and pouring cream.

CUMIN a spice also known as zeera or comino; has a spicy, nutty flavour.

CURRY LEAVES available fresh or dried and have a mild curry flavour; use like bay leaves.

CURRY PASTES some recipes in this book call for commercially prepared pastes of varying strengths and flavours. Use whichever one you feel best suits your spice-level tolerance.

korma paste a mix of mostly heat-free spices; forms the base of a mild, slightly nutty-tasting, slow-cooked curry.

powder a blend of ground spices including chilli, cinnamon, coriander, mace, fennel, cumin, fenugreek, cardamom and turmeric.

red curry paste a popular curry paste; a hot blend of red chilli, garlic, shallot, lemon grass, salt, galangal, shrimp paste, kaffir lime peel, coriander, cumin and paprika. It is milder than the hotter thai green curry paste.

rogan josh paste a medium-hot blend that is a specialty of Kashmir in northern India. It contains tomatoes, fenugreek, coriander, paprika and cumin.

EGGPLANT also known as aubergine.

baby also known as finger or japanese eggplant; very small and slender.

thai also known as makeua prao, golf-ball sized eggplants available in different colours but most commonly green traced in off-white; crisper than the common purple variety, they have bitter seeds that must be removed before using.

FENUGREEK a member of the pea family, the seeds have a bitter taste; the ground seeds are used in Indian curries, powders and pastes.

FIVE-SPICE POWDER (chinese five-spice) a fragrant mixture of ground cinnamon, cloves, star anise, sichuan pepper and fennel seeds.

FLOUR

cornflour also known as cornstarch; used as a thickening agent. Available as 100% corn (maize) and wheaten cornflour.

plain all-purpose flour made from wheat.

self-raising (self-rising) plain flour sifted with baking powder in the proportion of 1 cup flour to 2 teaspoons baking powder.

GAI LAN also known as chinese broccoli, gai larn, kanah, gai lum and chinese kale; appreciated more for its stems than its coarse leaves.

GALANGAL a rhizome with a hot ginger-citrusy flavour; used similarly to ginger and garlic. Use fresh ginger if unavailable.

GARAM MASALA a blend of spices that includes cardamom, cinnamon, coriander, cloves, fennel and cumin. Black pepper and chilli can be added for heat.

GHEE a type of clarified butter where the milk solids are cooked until they are a golden brown, which imparts a nutty flavour and sweet aroma; ghee can be heated to a high temperature without burning. Often used in Indian cooking. Available from the refrigerated section of some supermarkets and from Indian grocery stores.

GINGER also known as green or root ginger; the thick root of a tropical plant.

ground also known as powdered ginger; used as a flavouring in cakes and pies but cannot be substituted for fresh ginger.

GRANITA BISCUITS contain wheat flakes, have a crumbly texture and are easy to digest. Digestives, Shredded Wheatmeal and Graham Crackers may be substituted.

GRAVY POWDER an instant gravy mix made with browned flour. Plain flour can be used instead for thickening. Available from supermarkets in a variety of flavours.

HARISSA a Moroccan paste made from dried chillies, cumin, garlic, oil and caraway seeds. Available from Middle-Eastern food shops and some supermarkets.

HORSERADISH CREAM a paste of grated horseradish, mustard seeds, oil and sugar.

KAFFIR LIME LEAVES also known as bai magrood, sold fresh, dried or frozen; looks like two glossy dark green leaves joined end to end, forming a rounded hourglass shape. A strip of fresh lime peel may be substituted for each kaffir lime leaf.

KITCHEN STRING made of a natural product such as cotton or hemp so that it neither affects the flavour of the food it's tied around nor melts when heated.

KUMARA Polynesian name of an orange-fleshed sweet potato often confused with yam.

LAMB

forequarter chops cut from the shoulder end.

shanks, french-trimmed also known as drumsticks or frenched shanks; the gristle and narrow end of the bone is discarded then the remaining meat is trimmed.

shoulder cut from the shoulder. Is very hard to carve with the bone in; to make carving easier, butchers will bone it and sell it as a boneless rolled shoulder.

LEEK looks like a giant green onion but is more mild in flavour.

baby, or pencil leeks, are young, slender leeks; they are available early in the growing season.

LENTILS (red, brown, yellow) dried pulses identified by and named after their colour.

MARSALA a sweet, fortified wine to which additional alcohol has been added, most commonly in the form of brandy. Available in a range of styles, from sweet to dry.

MINCE also known as ground meat.

MIXED DRIED FRUIT a mix of sultanas, raisins, currants, mixed peel and cherries.

MIXED SPICE a blend of ground spices, usually cinnamon, allspice and nutmeg.

MOROCCAN SEASONING available from most Middle-Eastern food stores, spice shops and major supermarkets. A blend of turmeric, cinnamon and cumin add a Moroccan flavour to cooking.

MUSHROOMS

button small, cultivated white mushrooms.

enoki has clumps of long, spaghetti-like stems with tiny, snowy white caps.

oyster also known as abalone; grey-white mushrooms shaped like a fan. Prized for their smooth texture and their subtle, oyster-like flavour.

portobello these are mature swiss browns. Large, dark brown mushrooms with full-bodied flavour, ideal for filling or barbecuing.

shiitake when fresh are also known as chinese black, forest or golden oak mushrooms. Are large and meaty and, although cultivated, have the earthiness and taste of wild mushrooms.

swiss brown also known as cremini or roman mushrooms, light brown mushrooms having a full bodied flavour. Button or cup mushrooms can be substituted.

MUSSELS must be tightly closed when bought, indicating they are alive. Before cooking, scrub the shells with a strong brush and remove the 'beards'. Some mussels might not open – you do not have to discard these, just open with a knife and cook a little more if you wish.

MUSTARD

dijon pale brown, distinctively flavoured, fairly mild-tasting french mustard.

seeds, black also known as brown mustard seeds; more pungent than the yellow (or white) seeds used in prepared mustards.

wholegrain also known as seeded. A french-style coarse-grain mustard made from crushed mustard seeds and dijon-style french mustard.

NOODLES, RAMEN Japanese instant-style deep-fried wheat noodles. May be fat, thin or ribbon-like, as well as straight or wrinkled. Similar to the instant 2-minute noodles found in supermarkets.

OILS

olive made from ripened olives. Extra virgin and virgin are the best, while extra light or light refers to taste, not fat levels.

peanut pressed from ground peanuts; most commonly used oil in Asian cooking because of its high smoke point (capacity to handle high heat without burning).

sesame roasted, crushed, white sesame seeds; a flavouring rather than a cooking medium.

vegetable sourced from plants.

ONIONS

baby also known as pickling and cocktail onions; are baby brown onions, though are larger than shallots. To peel, cover with boiling water and stand for 2 minutes, then drain. The skins will slip off easily.

green also known as scallion or, incorrectly, shallot; an immature onion picked before the bulb has formed, has a long, bright-green stalk.

shallots also called french or golden shallots or eschalots; small and brown-skinned.

spring an onion with a small white bulb and long, narrow green-leafed tops.

PANCETTA see pork.

PATTY-PAN SQUASH also known as crookneck or custard marrow pumpkins; a round, slightly flat summer squash being yellow to pale-green in colour and having a scalloped edge. It has a firm white flesh and a distinct flavour.

PISTACHIOS delicately flavoured green nuts inside hard off-white shells. We always use shelled nuts in our recipes.

POLENTA also known as cornmeal; a ground, flour-like cereal made of dried corn (maize). Also the name of the dish made from it.

PORK

ham hock the lower portion of the leg; includes the meat, fat and bone. Most have been cured, smoked or both.

neck sometimes called pork scotch; a boneless cut from the foreloin.

pancetta an Italian unsmoked bacon; pork belly cured in salt and spices then rolled into a sausage shape and dried for several weeks. Used, sliced or chopped, as an ingredient rather than eaten on its own.

prosciutto cured, unsmoked, pressed ham.

sausage, italian pork available as both sweet, which is flavoured with garlic and fennel seed, and hot, which has chilli.

shoulder joint sold with the bone in or out.

spare ribs (american-style spareribs); well-trimmed mid-loin ribs.

POTATOES, BABY NEW also known as chats; not a separate variety but an early harvest with very thin skin.

PRAWNS also known as shrimp.

PRESERVED LEMON RIND a North African specialty; lemons are quartered and preserved in salt and lemon juice or water. To use, remove and discard pulp. Squeeze juice from rind, then rinse well and slice thinly. Sold in delicatessens and major supermarkets.

RAISINS dried sweet grapes.

RAITA a minted yogurt and cucumber dish. It is a cooling accompaniment to fiery curries.

RAS EL HANOUT a classic spice blend used in Moroccan cooking. The name means 'top of the shop' and is the very best spice blend a spice merchant has to offer. Most versions contain over a dozen spices, including cardamom, nutmeg, mace, cinnamon and ground chilli.

RICE

basmati a white, fragrant long-grained rice. Wash several times before cooking.

medium-grain previously sold as calrose rice; an extremely versatile rice that can be substituted for short- or long-grain rices.

RISONI small, rice-shaped pasta similar to orzo; used in soups and salads.

ROMANO CHEESE a hard, sheep- or cow's-milk cheese. Straw-coloured and grainy in texture. Substitute with parmesan.

SAUCES

char siu a Chinese barbecue sauce made from sugar, water, salt, fermented soya bean paste, honey, soy sauce, malt syrup and spices. Found at most supermarkets.

fish also called nam pla or nuoc nam; made from pulverised salted fermented fish, most often anchovies. Has a very pungent smell and strong taste, so use sparingly.

oyster Asian in origin, a rich, brown sauce made from oysters and their brine, cooked with salt and soy, and thickened with starches.

soy also known as sieu, made from fermented soya beans. Several variations are available in most supermarkets and Asian food stores. We use a mild Japanese variety in our recipes; possibly the best table soy and the one to choose if you only want one variety.

light soy a fairly thin, pale but salty tasting sauce; used in dishes in which the natural colour of the ingredients is to be maintained. Not to be confused with salt-reduced or low-sodium soy sauces.

tamari a thick, dark soy sauce made mainly from soya beans, but without the wheat used in most standard soy sauces.

tomato pasta a blend of tomatoes, herbs and spices.

worcestershire a dark-coloured condiment made from garlic, soy sauce, tamarind, onions, molasses, lime, anchovies, vinegar and seasonings.

SAUSAGES minced meat seasoned with salt and spices, mixed with cereal and packed into casings. Also known as snags or bangers.

SILVER BEET also known as swiss chard and mistakenly called spinach; a member of the beet family grown for its tasty green leaves and celery-like stems. Best cooked rather than eaten raw. Also known as blettes.

SOUR CREAM a thick commercially-cultured soured cream. Minimum fat content 35%.

SPLIT PEAS a variety of yellow or green pea grown specifically for drying. When dried, the peas usually split along a natural seam. Whole and split dried peas are available packaged in supermarkets and in bulk in health-food stores.

STAR ANISE dried star-shaped pod having an astringent aniseed flavour; used to favour stocks and marinades. Available whole and ground, it is an essential ingredient in five-spice powder.

SUGAR

caster also known as superfine or finely granulated table sugar.

dark brown a moist, dark brown sugar with a rich flavour due to natural molasses syrup.

light brown a soft, finely granulated sugar retaining molasses for its colour and flavour.

white a coarsely granulated table sugar, also known as crystal sugar.

SULTANAS dried grapes that are also known as golden raisins.

TAMARI see sauces.

TAMARIND CONCENTRATE the distillation of tamarind pulp into a condensed, compacted paste with a sweet-sour, slightly astringent taste. Thick and purple-black, it requires no soaking. Found in Asian food stores.

TURMERIC, GROUND a member of the ginger family, its root is dried and ground, resulting in the rich yellow powder that gives many Indian dishes their characteristic yellow colour. It is intensely pungent in taste, but not hot.

VINEGAR

balsamic made from the juice of Trebbiano grapes; is a deep brown colour with a sweet and sour flavour.

white balsamic is a clear and lighter version of balsamic vinegar; it has a fresh, sweet, clean taste.

brown malt made from fermented malt and beech shavings.

cider (apple) made from fermented apples.

white made from the spirit of cane sugar.

white wine made from a white wine blend.

WHITE SWEET POTATO is less sweet than kumara; has an earthy flavour and a purple flesh beneath its white skin. is best baked.

ZUCCHINI also known as courgette. A small green, yellow or white vegetable; part of the squash family.

Conversion Chart

MEASURES

One Australian metric measuring cup holds approximately 250ml; one Australian metric tablespoon holds 20ml; one Australian metric teaspoon holds 5ml.

The difference between one country's measuring cups and another's is within a two- or three-teaspoon variance, and will not affect your cooking results.

North America, New Zealand and the United Kingdom use a 15ml tablespoon.

All cup and spoon measurements are level. The most accurate way of measuring dry ingredients is to weigh them. When measuring liquids, use a clear glass or plastic jug with the metric markings.

We use large eggs with an average weight of 60g.

DRY MEASURES

METRIC	IMPERIAL
15g	½oz
30g	1oz
60g	2oz
90g	3oz
125g	4oz (¼lb)
155g	5oz
185g	6oz
220g	7oz
250g	8oz (½lb)
280g	9oz
315g	10oz
345g	11oz
375g	12oz (¾lb)
410g	13oz
440g	14oz
470g	15oz
500g	16oz (1lb)
750g	24oz (1½lb)
1kg	32oz (2lb)

LIQUID MEASURES

METRIC	IMPERIAL
30ml	1 fluid oz
60ml	2 fluid oz
100ml	3 fluid oz
125ml	4 fluid oz
150ml	5 fluid oz
190ml	6 fluid oz
250ml	8 fluid oz
300ml	10 fluid oz
500ml	16 fluid oz
600ml	20 fluid oz
1000ml (1 litre)	1¾ pints

LENGTH MEASURES

METRIC	IMPERIAL
3mm	⅛in
6mm	¼in
1cm	½in
2cm	¾in
2.5cm	1in
5cm	2in
6cm	2½in
8cm	3in
10cm	4in
13cm	5in
15cm	6in
18cm	7in
20cm	8in
23cm	9in
25cm	10in
28cm	11in
30cm	12in (1ft)

OVEN TEMPERATURES

These oven temperatures are only a guide for conventional ovens. For fan-forced ovens, check the manufacturer's manual.

	°C (CELSIUS)	°F (FAHRENHEIT)	GAS MARK
Very slow	120	250	½
Slow	150	275-300	1-2
Moderately slow	160	325	3
Moderate	180	350-375	4-5
Moderately hot	200	400	6
Hot	220	425-450	7-8
Very hot	240	475	9

Index

Published in 2012 by ACP Books, Sydney.
ACP Books are published by ACP Magazines Limited,
a division of Nine Entertainment Co.
54 Park St, Sydney
GPO Box 4088, Sydney, NSW 2001.
phone (02) 9282 8618; fax (02) 9267 9438
acpbooks@acpmagazines.com.au; www.acpbooks.com.au

ACP BOOKS

General Manager - Christine Whiston

Editor-in-Chief - Susan Tomnay

Creative Director - Hieu Chi Nguyen

Food Director - Pamela Clark

Published and Distributed in the United Kingdom by Octopus Publishing Group

Endeavour House

189 Shaftesbury Avenue

London WC2H 8JY

United Kingdom

phone (+44)(0)207 632 5400; fax (+44)(0)207 632 5405

info@octopus-publishing.co.uk;

www.octopusbooks.co.uk

Printed by C&C Offset Printing, China.

International foreign language rights, Brian Cearnes, ACP Books bcearnes@acpmagazines.com.au

A catalogue record for this book is available from the British Library.
ISBN: 978-1-74245-263-0 (hbk.)

© ACP Magazines Ltd 2012
ABN 18 053 273 546